The Wonderful WIZARD in YoU!

The
Wonderful
WIZARD
Y in oU!

SIDNEY FRIEDMAN

PELICAN PUBLISHING COMPANY
Gretna 1999

The word "Pelican" and the depiction of a pelican are trademarks
of Pelican Publishing Co., Inc.,
and are registered in the U.S. Patent and Trademark Office.

Library of Congress Cataloging-in-Publication Data

Friedman, Sidney.
 The Wonderful Wizard in You! / by Sidney Friedman.
  p. cm.
 ISBN 1-56554-391-2 (alk. paper)
 1. Success. I. Title.
BJ1611.F84 1999
158.1—dc21   99-12025
                                               CIP

Printed in the United States of America

Published by Pelican Publishing Company, Inc.
1000 Burmaster Street, Gretna, Louisiana 70053

For decades the story of Dorothy's quest to get back to her home in Kansas has given faithful service to the young in heart—and time, technology, and $100 million Hollywood budgets have been powerless to put the tale's kindly philosophy and heartfelt wisdom out of fashion.

To my wife, Sue; my daughters, Wendi and Lori; to the loving memory of my Mom and Dad; to my friend Frank Freudberg; and to L. Frank Baum—the genius who invented Oz—and especially to those of you who have been faithful to *The Wizard of Oz* in return; and to all those who truly believe they are young in heart, I dedicate this book.

Contents

The
Wonderful
WIZARD
Y in oU!

SID FRIEDMAN

A Letter To You

Date: The first day of the rest of your life . . .

Dear Reader:

For Dorothy, her trip from Kansas to Oz and back home again is a wonderful expedition filled with difficult lessons, astonishing self-discovery, and ultimately, a genuine sense of joy and self-confidence she had never before experienced.

But much more than that, it isn't until *after* Dorothy gets home that her truly amazing adventure—the rest of her life—begins, because she now has access to the most important thing in the world: She has an unshakable confidence in her own power to achieve virtually *anything* she sets her heart and mind on.

Do you remember the scene from the end of *The Wizard of Oz* movie that takes place just after the balloon that the Wizard is going to take Dorothy back to Kansas in takes off without her? Dorothy is quite distraught, and Glinda the Good Witch appears. Dorothy practically begs Glinda to help her get back home, but Glinda smiles wisely and tells her that she's always had to power to get back to Kansas herself. Scarecrow asks why Glinda didn't tell Dorothy sooner. And again, Glinda smiles again and says that Dorothy had to learn it for herself.

"She had to learn it for herself." Ain't it the truth; ain't it the truth! Don't we *all* have to learn things for ourselves before we really come to believe them? I know that's how it works in me.

Through this book, it is my goal to help you discover, like Dorothy, that you too have an absolutely, undeniably *incredible* source of

THE BELLEVUE • FOURTH FLOOR • BROAD AT WALNUT • PHILADELPHIA • PA 19102 • 215-875-8707

SID FRIEDMAN

strength, creativity and self-discipline that you can begin putting to work for you today.

Right now. *This very minute.* If you let it, *The Wonderful Wizard in You!* can help you find—and tap into—that power you have inside.

Best wishes,

Sid Friedman

P.S. When you get to the last page of *The Wonderful Wizard in You!*, you'll see the last two words are not *The End.* Instead, they read *The Beginning,* because that's what I hope you'll experience then—the start of your own amazing adventure down the road of life to wherever it is you want to go. Good luck!

Take the Dorothy Challenge!

The amazing, incredible story of *The Wizard of Oz!*

Of course, it's all a fairy tale. Everyone knows that.

But doesn't it make sense that if *The Wizard of Oz*'s Dorothy can wake up (after being knocked half out of this world by a tornado) and manage to get her bearings, continue to be a kind person, and achieve her heart's desire—doesn't it make sense that you, too, can figure out a way to get whatever it is you want?

Well, I *know* it's true. I know it because it's happened to me. I figured out my way to get what I want. I got knocked down and dragged out by life, and I came back, maybe a little worse for wear, but I also came back smarter and stronger than ever.

And you can, too.

I plan on showing you how. Not in vague, general terms. Not in a "rah-rah" pep-rally style. Not with a bunch of empty, feel-good sayings and clichéd advice.

I'm going to show you what I did and how I did it in a way that you can adopt to your own style. And you are going to be so successful that you won't believe it's happening to you.

But, before we get started, I'm going to ask you to accept "The Dorothy Challenge."

And boy, will you think I have some nerve, because I'm going to ask you to write a check for *$1,000* and send it where I tell you.

I know you just paid several dollars for this book, and here I am already hitting you up for more money.

But don't worry, I'm not selling you anything. You already bought the book. The extra grand is for the Make-A-Wish charitable foundation for dying kids that I help manage, and I bet that 365 days from today, you'll send that foundation a check for $1,000—and you'll do it gladly.

No way?

Don't be so sure.

Write today's date right here in the book: _____.

Now, make a note in your daily planner (if you don't have a daily planner . . . well, we'll deal with that later in the book) that one year from today you are going to call Sid Friedman in Philadelphia. Here's my number: 800-896-2213.

Now, here's what's going on. I want to make a personal promise to you: If you follow the success formula presented in this book, if you run with the lessons available in *The Wizard of Oz,* you will make so much money during the next twelve months that you really will call me up one year from today and you'll tell me personally, "Sid, believe it or not, one year ago I bought your book, and to make a long story short, today's the day I'm mailing the check!"

No way?

Just keep reading.

It's Always Darkest . . .

It was almost twenty years ago.

Thursday, March 22, 1980, to be exact.

It was freezing out, just after 7 in the morning.

I had just walked out of Dr. Louis Carp's office at Pennsylvania Hospital in Philadelphia. He had told me something I didn't want to hear. He had told me I had cancer behind my left eye.

I couldn't believe it.

"You don't have very many choices," he said. "As a matter of fact, only two. You can either save your left eye and lose your life, or you can lose your left eye and save your life. Your choice. We need to kill the cancer with radiation—and the unavoidable side effect is that you will be blind in the left eye."

"Those are my two choices?" I asked.

"Yes," he said.

It took me about an eighth of a second to think about it.

"OK," I said. "Go ahead. Do it. We'll sacrifice my eye."

And he did it.

I took radiation therapy every day for seventy-six straight days—a direct blast into my eye. I hated it. It was painful, nauseating, scary. But I hated that cancer more than the radiation, and that gave me determination. *I was going to beat the cancer.*

It worked.

The cancer went into remission and I recovered. And because I had learned to fight, I went on to be better and stronger and more successful than ever before.

But all that didn't give me my vision back.

It's true that I still had vision in one eye. I was even able to drive (I joked that I could only make right turns!). I was constantly worried that I'd get poked in my good eye or get into some kind of accident and lose all my sight. The prospect of becoming totally blind terrified me.

So, every four months, without fail, for sixteen years I went to the doctor for a checkup and said, "When am I going to get my sight back?"

He said, "You won't. Stop worrying about it. You made a good trade. Vision in one eye for your whole life. Be grateful."

Somehow, I had known to never quit asking for what I wanted.

Where had I learned that? Something was gnawing at me, tugging at the back of my mind.

Where had I learned that to stop *asking* is to stop wanting?

Trying to figure it out was driving me crazy.

Fast forward to March of 1996, the date of one of my regularly scheduled visits to Dr. Carp.

I asked him the question he'd heard sixty or seventy times before, and I expected his standard answer.

"When am I going to get my sight back?"

But this time, he looked up and he said, "You know, Sid, there *is* a new surgical technique just developed. Maybe we can try it. Because of the way your cataract has formed over the years, it might be worth a try."

And do you know what? . . .

It's always darkest right before dawn.

They tried the surgical technique on a Tuesday, and the next day, as they were getting ready to remove the bandages, Dr. Carp had a warning for me:

"Be prepared, Sidney. There's going be a flood of light coming right at you from your left eye. It'll be intense. That eye is not used to anything but darkness."

Remember, I hadn't seen a particle of light in that eye for seventeen years.

Then he takes the bandages off.

Bingo!

Wow!

Boy! He was right. *Intense* wasn't the word for it.

It was like they were shining an airport control tower's beacon light directly into my eye.

I could definitely see light, but I couldn't see clearly.

My eye was covered with medicine and drops and all kinds of stuff they put in it before, during, and after surgery. I could see light right away, but it took a lot of blinking and flushing out before I could see clearly.

But I could see clearly after a while.

And do you know what? The vision now back in my left eye was sharper and clearer than the vision in my right eye.

Now, how did that happen?

How did I get my vision back, after all that time and after I had listened to my doctor repeat those words, "Sorry, Sid, it just can't happen."?

I'm not sure, and neither is Dr. Carp.

But I think maybe I do know.

I think my dad, long departed, may have had something to do with it.

I think they were having a board of directors meeting or something up in heaven and someone said, "Any new business?" And my dad, Ben, raised his hand and said, "Well, my son's having eye surgery today. Can we give him his vision back?" And I guess the good Lord said "OK"—because now I can see, and no one can explain why.

And something else dawned on me.

It came to me in a flash. Maybe it was all that bright light.

I suddenly remembered where I had learned to never quit asking for what I wanted.

I remembered where I had learned that to stop *asking* is to stop *wanting.*

I remembered learning it from Dorothy in *The Wizard of Oz.*

"I want to get back to Kansas. I want to get back to Kansas. I want to get back to Kansas." She wouldn't shut up about it.

And do you know what? It worked!

Just like with my eye!

So, between a little girl named Dorothy in *The Wizard of Oz,* and my mom, Ceil, and my dad, Ben, and Dorothy's dog, Toto, and all the others she met along the Yellow Brick Road, I learned that *if you believe and believe and believe,* you really can tap into the power of the Wizard we all have inside us.

I learned that sink-your-teeth-in-and-never-let-go determination.

And I learned that if *you* never let up, if *you* keep on fighting back—the way Dorothy did, the way I did—if *you* keep on keeping on, if *you* never let go, *you* really *can* have whatever you want.

As long as you know what you want clearly, there's no doubt you can have it. And that's what this book is all about—getting whatever your dream is.

What Dorothy Learns

At the end of the story, Glinda the Good Witch proves that Dorothy has always possessed the power she needs to return to Kansas. Dorothy's problem all along isn't whether or not she has the power—her problem is believing that she has it.

When you think of Dorothy, what images come to mind?
"What a cute kid."
"What a sweet little kid."
"What a bright, precocious kid."
Yeah. Me too.
Except for one little problem: *I think she is completely nuts.*
Off her rocker. Stone cold crazy. Certifiably insane.
But *absolutely* brilliant!
And she *is* crazy.
Crazy like a fox.
When Dorothy gets an idea into her head, the risks, consequences, obstacles, even the likelihood of failure, are never even given a second thought.
That kind of impulsive, damn-the-torpedoes-full-speed-ahead behavior is insane.
The same kind of "insane" they called the Wright brothers, Thomas Edison, Albert Einstein, Bill Gates, and thousands of others who have achieved greatness.
Dorothy has inborn knowledge about dreaming a dream, making a plan, and never letting up. In this book, we're going to take a close look at what she does and how she does it, so that her strategy will be something that you can adapt to your situation—so that you will be able to get to your own Kansas.

18

Dorothy is so filled with 100 percent U.S.-certified pure determination, she never even thinks once about all the consequences that will follow when she grabs her dog Toto and runs away from home. Toto is in jeopardy, and that is all she needs to know. Her dog means everything to her, and she aims to protect him.

At any cost.

You know, ever since I was a little kid, I have been fascinated with the story of *The Wizard of Oz.*

For many years I didn't know why that story was so intriguing. I just knew it hypnotized me. Today (and I'm sixty-four), I know very, very clearly why that story rang so true to me. And by the end of this book, you'll know why it means so much to you, too.

Now, virtually everyone *thinks* they know of Dorothy of *Wizard of Oz* fame. But how many of you know the *real* Dorothy Gale (at least as real as a fictional character can get)?

What makes her tick? You see, the more you learn about Dorothy Gale, the more you are going to know about yourself.

You watch as situations arise in Dorothy's life similar to things that have happened (and will continue to happen) to you.

I know for a fact they've happened to me—and that's why I'm so sure they've happened to everyone I know.

Wizard Wisdom: *Watching* The Wizard of Oz *film reminded me that all along I had the power of believing right inside. I realized that there is no Wizard—except the one that's inside of you!*

The Sky's the Limit—
Even If There Is a Tornado Up There!

There is only one success—to be able to spend your life in your own way.

—Christopher Morley

How successful do you really want to be? Think about it: How successful do you really, *really* want to be?

Take *The Wizard of Oz*'s Dorothy, for example. Because of Dorothy's unrelenting perseverance in the face of truly impossible odds, she was able to return to Kansas and help her friends get their hearts' desires.

And you can do the same thing. Go ahead, name it—the sky's the limit. There is no doubt about it. You can absolutely, positively learn how to be successful beyond your wildest dreams—no matter what.

This book will give you *hundreds* of specific ideas, strategies, and techniques that I have used—and keep on using—to be successful. Some of these ideas, strategies, and techniques are complex—it takes pages and pages to describe them. Others are short and sweet—a simple phrase or sentence.

But whatever their length, they are all worth their weight in platinum.

It doesn't matter if you have some serious limitations (I certainly do!). It doesn't matter if you've tried and failed one thousand times before. There isn't a computer on the planet powerful enough to keep track of all the mistakes I've made—and even continue to make.

It doesn't even matter if circumstances around you make you think you can not succeed. I overcame tremendous obstacles.

You absolutely, positively can succeed.

I can prove it.

I guarantee it works.

I am living proof of the success system that has made me a successful man, and better than that, my success puts me in a position where I can do whatever I want to do. Any time, any thing, any place. I don't have to work—I love to work!

Why? What kind of a lunatic works when he doesn't have to?

I'll tell you what kind: the kind who loves what he does. Yes, I make a lot of money. But that's only the tip of the iceberg. I also help people—in my profession and beyond it—and that makes it all worthwhile.

I help run a charitable foundation.

I hang out with my family.

I speak to audiences all over the world and help them learn how to be as successful as they want to be.

The Twelve Greatest Scenes
from *The Wizard of Oz*

In my personal opinion, there are twelve scenes in *The Wizard of Oz* movie that are just fantastic.

Everyone I know has their own favorite scenes. These are mine. You'll instantly recognize them.

This is cool: Pay attention to how your brain replays these movie scenes—in color—right on the screen in the Theater of Your Mind. (By the way, although I call them "scenes," some of them are "sequences"—a series of related scenes.)

Great Scene #1

Dorothy possesses an instinctive courage to dream. Those of us who weren't born with it can learn to develop it

At the very beginning of the story we see Dorothy's absolute love for her dog Toto. Dorothy thinks that mean old Elmira Gulch has tried to harm her dog. Right away, she kneels down to examine him. She picks him up and runs to her home on the Gale farm, where she finds Aunt Em and Uncle Henry working on an old coal-oil five-hundred-chick incubator.

She breathlessly tells them what's happened.

Well, it looks like Dorothy has done what she has been taught: She goes to the supreme authorities—her aunt and uncle—but she doesn't get anywhere. They don't pay any attention to her. They are desperately trying to fix a broken-down old incubator and save hundreds of chicks from dying.

So Dorothy consults her friend Zeke, one of the farm hands.

Instead of helping, he tells her he's busy

But she's persistent, one of her great qualities. She asks for help from another one of the hands, Hunk.

He's no help either.

They are soon interrupted by Aunt Em, who tells the farm hands to get back to work.

Dorothy starts in again on Aunt Em. She's determined, no matter what the cost, to protect what she loves most: her dog Toto. Protecting Toto has become her primary goal. You'll see that she'll never let up.

Auntie Em isn't sympathetic. She admonishes Dorothy to stop imagining things—and insists Dorothy find a place where she won't get into any trouble.

That comment stops Dorothy cold.

She falls into deep thought, wondering about a place where there isn't any trouble. She asks Toto if there can be such a place. And then she begins singing "Over the Rainbow."

Many powerful insights repeat themselves throughout the story, and right here is another example of a great one: *You have to have the courage to dream.*

Dorothy makes a conscious effort to "find" that place where she needs to be. It's not nearby, it's far away, and somehow she realizes she can get there only on the wings of her dream.

How Successful Do You Really, *Really* Want to Be?

Everybody Wants to Be Successful—Or Do They?

Dorothy Gale has a goal. She wants—no, she needs—to get back home to Kansas.

Everybody has a goal. So, in a sense, everybody has a Kansas.

Do you know what yours is?

Do you believe you once bought a ticket to your version of Kansas? Do you believe you've been doing all the things that are required to get you where you want to go?

There are a lot of things you need to do in order to succeed, and not everybody really wants to do them. Do you think it is easy for Dorothy to face all of her fears and ask the Wizard of Oz to help her? No, but it is necessary. So she does it. And if you've seen the film, I'm sure you can recall her trembling in his presence.

I think this whole subject of success is like a seesaw when you're a kid. If you sit on one side, the other side goes up. If you think you want one thing, something else looks good.

It is a question of balance, counterbalance. You've got to give up something to get something. You can't have it all, but you should decide what it is you do want.

So, if you want to get that success, you've got to be prepared for hard work, discipline, and some frustration—all the things that we don't want to do but we know we have to do to get what we want.

I think more people don't make it—not because they're failures, but because they don't have a clear picture of succeeding or even of what they want.

The visualization of what they want is not clear.

And even if they know what they want, they're not willing to hold on tight for the whole period of time it takes to get it.

They won't hang in there until they reach the end.

It reminds me of the pump.

There's a water pump, and someone keeps pumping, pumping, pumping. Nothing happens.

"Ah! Forget it," he says, disgusted. He stops and walks away. Somebody else comes along, gives one good yank on the handle and—bingo!—the water gushes out in torrents.

I think that's the major difference between people who succeed and people who don't. Those who don't don't want to pay for their success.

They want it, they think, but they're not willing to pay for it.

The Controllable vs. the Uncontrollable.

You can't help it if your farmhouse falls on the Wicked Witch's sister. But you can control what you do when you're faced with the resulting crises.

When I ask the question "How successful do you really, really want to be?" what I'm really getting at is, "How well are you able to manage yourself?"

You can become as successful as you want to be—as long as you know how to take control of the controllable and have a backup plan for the uncontrollable.

Dorothy has an inborn knowledge about success. She just knows about dreaming a dream, making a plan, and never letting up. But remember, Dorothy's story is a fairy tale. Your life is real. Take the lessons from the fiction and make it into fact—make it into your life.

As Henry David Thoreau once said, "Things do not change, but we do."

Wizard Wisdom: Get a notebook and a pen or pencil and keep them with this book. Keep track of the ideas, insights, brainstorms, wishes, dreams, and goals that reading this book will cause to bubble up to the surface of your mind. Don't rely on your memory. Good ideas are perishable. Preserve them immediately when they materialize. Step back from what you do every day. Take a good look at where you are and where you want to go. Read with the idea in mind that you want to change how you go about your life.

The Fear of Success

Most people say they want to be successful, but I'm not sure in their heart of hearts that they really do want to be. Perhaps it has to do with the very real scariness of success.

Maybe people are afraid of being successful. Success brings many things, but one of the fundamental things that happens is that things change. Take the Scarecrow, for example. He'd rather have stayed impaled in the cornfield than deal with having to risk change.

People are used to a comfort zone. They are comfortable with what they are familiar with. They are comfortable with where they are now, and to break out of that comfort zone to go someplace else—even though it is someplace better or someplace good—they may be very scared about it.

There's a commitment that you have to make to want to be successful.

And that commitment is the thing that will drive your discipline if you keep the commitment up front in your mind at all times. It does have to do with the idea of dreaming in color, with knowing exactly what your dream is, what it looks like, and what it feels like. But there's a chance that when you get to where you want to go, you may be all alone. As you come closer and closer to making your dream real, there will be less and less people going with you. There are a lot of dropouts along the road to success. People run out of fuel, get flats, change direction, or like it where they find themselves even though they are only halfway to where they originally wanted to go.

Often, you're out there all alone, and sometimes that is pretty scary.

I believe that people have a fear of success even greater than their fear of failure. Everybody is used to the fear of failure. They've been brainwashed by themselves or others about the things they think they can't do and they believe it—and they act it out.

The instinct to succeed for Dorothy is 100 percent determination. She never even thinks once about all the consequences that will result from just grabbing her dog Toto and running away from home.

But the fear of success is an unknown territory. It's an unfamiliar fear, the most frightening kind of fear.

Some people tell me they don't believe the fear of success exists, but I certainly do. For one thing, if there wasn't a fear of success, more people would be successful, and more people would try to get there. But it's an unknown territory; it's uncharted water.

I can remember a time when I was really fearful. As a matter of fact, I was fearful for the first ten years I was in the insurance business. Before I got married I was with a family-owned business, and I was afraid to jump out. At first I didn't know what success looked like. So all I was able to see of it was what I could see from afar. I'd see a place I didn't even understand. It was a place that seemed impossible to get to, too.

It was more than that comfort-zone factor with me. I didn't understand success. I didn't know what it looked like. So even if I had stumbled upon it, I wouldn't have even known it.

But somewhere down the road, just about the time I got married, I left the family-owned business, I started to go on my own, and I had a little taste of success.

Apparently, for me, success bred more success. I got a little bit, and I wanted a little bit more. I got a little bit more, and I wanted even more. And then I wanted more, and so I worked for more. It began to build up. As success became part of my life, I found that it wasn't scary.

But it sure was in the beginning. It was the most unsettling place I had ever been to. I knew it meant that if I stayed there, everything that was familiar to me was going to change. I was nervous, even though I knew it was fun. I knew people who were successful. They had money, cars, homes, and buildings, but I didn't know what it was like.

And what else you had to pay to reach success.

I'm saying that I didn't know what price I had to pay to get there. Maybe that is the best definition of the fear of success: The price looked so steep that I didn't believe I could come up with the price of admission.

But I was never more wrong. I found out that I had enough for the ticket on me all along.

Discover What You Really Want

Dorothy knows clearly what it is she wants. That's the fairy-tale part. For the rest of us living in the real world, it isn't so easy.

To figure out what you want in life you have to reach deep down inside yourself and plumb for the answer.

Maybe you have to spend some time thinking about what you want to be and what you want to be *like.*

There's a sad but true fact that I often use in my speaking engagements: People spend more time planning their two-week summer vacations than they do planning their entire lives!

Think about that.

How many times have you and your family or you and your friends gathered around the kitchen table some Saturday afternoon with a notebook, travel brochures, guidebooks, and hotel directories and spent hours and hours figuring out how to squeeze the most value out of the two weeks and two thousand bucks you have for your annual vacation?

Now, how many times have to done the same thing in order to squeeze the most value out of the one thousand months that the average person lives?

Twice?

No?

Oh, then at least once?

No? Not even once? Never sat down and set a course for yourself? Never developed a plan?

Hmmmm! Maybe that explains why you are not as far along the road to Success as you'd like to be!

Maybe it's time to put the same effort into planning your life as you do in planning your vacation or arranging to get tickets for next week's ball game.

Plan that time and think about what you want to do.

If you feel like you are truly motivated to succeed but can't seem to organize yourself into doing something with that motivation and energy, don't be discouraged. Lots of successful people will tell you how at one time in their lives they too felt as if they were all dressed up with nowhere to go, too. They're revving their engines, but they are in the gear I call "Stuck." It's not "Drive" and it's not "Neutral" and it's not "Reverse." It's kind of a Twilight Zone ditch along the side of the road to Success. And the beautiful thing is, it's really simple to get out of.

You just need the right tools.

> ***Wizard Wisdom:*** *You might give aptitude testing a try. This kind of testing is a valid thing to do. You may have all the ingredients to be a natural at something, but for one reason or another, you have never consciously been able to put it all together. Aptitude testing can help you discover your talents. Maybe you have to find a career-counseling service in your city to give you some testing to identify where your strengths and special talents are, where do your interests lie, what you can do that won't seem like a drudgery.*

A lot of people are really on stuck.

I was on the podium once with a guy named Dr. John Compare, and John told the audience, "You have to have a job that you love. You have to have a career that you love. There's no point spending a whole lifetime doing something you don't like. It's not worth it. If you want to be happy for just one hour, take a nap. And if you want to be happy for a day, go fishing. If you want to be happy for a week, take a vacation. If you want to be happy for a month, get married. If you want to be happy for a year, inherit a fortune. But even after a year, after you acquire everything you can think of, you'll still wind up unhappy after you've bought everything you wanted if you're not really happy in what you do every day."

His point is, get yourself a job that you really love, do something that you're really in love with, *so that when you go to work every day, it will be going to be a place you really want to go to.*

That's a hard thing to do. Because most people come to work in the morning saying, "It's just a job," and they spend every day of their entire lives—sixty-five years—just waiting until they can stop working. And when they finally stop working, they realize life's over.

They've been waiting for this time to come, and when it does, they are terribly disappointed.

I suggest that you really find out how successful you want to be—however you want to define success—during, not after, the journey. Now, not at the end. The end is too late. In the end, you turn in your badge and go home.

You want to do it while you've still got the badge, so you can go through your whole life enjoying that journey from the moment you wake up in the morning until you close your eyes at the end of every day you've lived to the fullest.

You think I'm kidding? I'm not.

I'm deadly serious.

Life is a very difficult, very challenging thing. There are a million disappointments, tragedies, misfortunes, and inequities. Good people who devote their lives to helping others sometimes die young in senseless accidents, while rotten, greedy, cruel people live on almost forever, making misery everywhere they go.

That's even more of a reason why you should work hard to be successful, to carry on the fight, to win one for the good guys.

It can be a fun journey to somewhere you want to be.

I think once you begin loving what you do, once you begin to have a good time doing what you do, once you actually begin to want to do what you do, the fish will begin to jump in the boat for you.

Find a way to have a great time doing what you do, and I bet that's where you'll find success, because what you are doing will be so much fun, good fortune and prosperity will just come to you.

I don't believe in intuition. When you get sudden
flashes of perception, it is just the brain working faster
than usual. But you've been getting ready to know it for a
long time, and when it comes, you feel you've known it always.

—Katherine Anne Porter

Great Scene #2

Dorothy gets the ruby slippers. The ruby slippers represent Dorothy's ability to *believe* (a power the Wicked Witch doesn't want Dorothy to have), and Glinda's warning to "keep tight inside of them" is crucial advice.

Once Dorothy's tornado-ravaged farmhouse lands in Oz, Glinda arrives and identifies herself as the Good Witch of the North.

She then gives Dorothy the lowdown: The Munchkins have summoned Glinda because, they have told her, a new witch has just dropped a house on the Wicked Witch of the East.

The Munchkins are pleased with that development. The powerful Wicked Witch had long ago enslaved them. And now, as a result of where the house has fallen, the only things left of the Wicked Witch of the East are two glittery ruby slippers.

The Munchkins appear, and Dorothy is proclaimed the national heroine of Munchkin country.

But the festivities suddenly halt when a burst of red smoke and flash appears right at Dorothy's feet.

This is bad news: The Wicked Witch of the West, sister of the recently deceased Wicked Witch of the East, has arrived, and she's not happy. She seems to accept the death of her sister readily enough, but she has become obsessed with getting a hold of the ruby slippers for herself. Just as she is about to take hold of them—*presto!*—they vanish from her hands!

The Wicked Witch screeches that the slippers have

disappeared. She demands Dorothy return them. But Glinda interrupts her tirade and tells her it's too late— the slippers are now on Dorothy's feet.

This exchange frightens Dorothy, and the scene ends with the Wicked Witch demanding the slippers and screaming that she's the only one who knows how to use them.

Tune in to Your Intuition

Your gut is a good compass to use when trying to find your direction. And it works if you are in Philadelphia, San Francisco, Geneva, Istanbul—or Oz.

Think about how Dorothy tunes in to the value of befriending the Lion, the Scarecrow, and the Tin Man. She knows they'll be able to help each other.

A lot of intuitive direction depends on how well you can focus and develop your natural psychic ability. I'm not talking about astrology or fortune-telling or people who help the police find clues to murders. I'm talking about that natural wisdom we all have buried deeply inside.

Most people have a great deal of psychic ability. They just don't know it.

To give you an example of what I am talking about, have you ever had a premonition? You say, "Gee—I wonder how old so-and-so's doing! I haven't talked to him in years!"

Then, all of a sudden, the phone rings, and guess who? It's old so-and-so! You get a little nervous because you have no idea where that hunch came from, but it was so clear, so definite, that you know there's got to be some more where that came from. You try to conjure that psychic energy up again, but you can't repeat it. You don't know enough about it to get it under harness.

Or, how about when you are walking down the street, looking all around, and suddenly, for no reason you know of, you look down— just in time to see a hole in the sidewalk.

Why?

Because we are all aware of much more information unconsciously than we know about consciously.

The fact is that most people do have some psychic ability. It seems as if our bellies are somehow in better communication with our intuition than the rest of us.

What goes on in your belly is usually much better than what goes on in your head. What goes on in your head is logical; what goes on in your belly is emotional.

Sometimes you know what to do or how to react better by what your belly tells you than by what your head tells you. Sometimes you have to listen to your belly. Even though your head says, "Don't," your belly says, "Do." Try listening to your belly, as long as it's not illegal, immoral, or fattening.

Take a chance.

Your belly probably has better instincts, more education, than your brain. Your brain has been around only as long as you have. But what fuels your intuition may be something bigger, much bigger, than that. Remember the telephone call from old so-and-so. Well, whatever provided you with that hunch probably comes from a source bigger than any one of us.

Your belly has the benefit of something extraordinary, but your thoughts come from an ordinary brain. Your belly has much more going for it.

You probably have something in your belly that is psychic that tells you what to do, and you're right. But it's your responsibility to quiet yourself down enough to be able to tune in to that source.

It was this kind of a gut feeling that Dorothy follows that leads her to the Wizard, who ultimately leads her to achieve her heart's desire.

I know that I have done more right things with my belly than with my head.

Sometimes my head gives me stop signs. I get these red signals in front of me that say, "Sid, don't do it." But my belly's saying, "It's green, man, go. Don't listen to your brain."

Insight from Oz: *When I've gone ahead full blast, it's usually worked out for me. And when I haven't, when I've hesitated, I've fallen on my head. So, as far as I'm concerned, listening to my belly is the better strategy.*

Rule 80/20/100/51

Dorothy doesn't know everything about getting to Oz—just the general direction. Yet, as it turns out, that was good enough.

There's a rule that I live by that helps me with my belly rather than my head.

I call this rule "The 80/20/100/51 Rule."

And it applies whenever a situation comes up that needs some careful consideration. Whenever anything comes up in my mind—a belly vs. a head decision—here's what I do, and here's what I recommend for you:

> **Wizard Wisdom:** *Spend 20 percent of your time on any particular project gathering 80 percent of the facts you need. Then, when you get 80 percent of the information . . . make a decision 100 percent of the time . . . and hope you are right 51 percent of the time.*

Most people do the opposite of that rule. They spend 20 percent of their time gathering 80 percent of the facts. At that point, their heads say to them "Get the other 20 percent—you have to get the last 20 percent—don't go on until you have every last drop of the information." Then they spend the last 80 percent of the available time trying to gather all of that small percentage, that 20 percent, but they can never get it all, so they never get to a point where they can make a decision because they never have 100 percent.

And if you never make a decision, how can you ever be right?

So what I'm saying is when I spend 20 percent of my time, I get 80 percent of the facts under my belt. My belly takes over and says "Forget your head; go with me. Eighty percent is enough."

Make a decision right away, 100 percent of the time, and you know what? Even though I'm only going for 51 percent, I'm right 99 percent of the time.

Why? Because my belly knows more than my head. I'm convinced that that is probably what motivates lots of top executives, business owners, really successful people. Their bellies, not their brains.

> **Insight from Oz:** *There's really something to the art of going with your belly. Learn to listen to it and it'll pay you back generously.*

Words from the Wise
Valuable insights about the journey—from successful people

I grew up as an Italian kid in East Harlem, and I was the only white kid on the block. We were not wealthy, but I was never told that I wasn't worthy. If I came home with a "C" report card, I was encouraged by my parents. They'd say, "That's good, but you can try a little harder.

I was never derided or put down. I tell you this in retrospect. No ten- or eleven-year-old kid can understand it when it's happening, but the impact of encouragement—or discouragement—can be powerful, and people carry the effects into adulthood.

My parents made tremendous sacrifice to send me to Holy Cross College in Worcester, Massachusetts. I was going to classes five and a half days a week. Other kids went to their schools three or four days, in dungarees. I wore a tie and jacket.

The primary causes of my success are my parents, my wife, my education, and the Marine Corps. In the corps I learned how to deal with that 10 percent of all people who never get seem to want to understand anything, and how to look people in the eye and give them bad news when I have to.

When it comes to my wife, I can't say enough in praise of her. I was never a success in the material world until I got married. She encouraged me and never quit. She picked up at age thirty where my parents left off.

No one ever told me I couldn't do it. And when they told me I could do it, I believed them, and it all came true!

Joe Cassale
Phoenix Home Life
Norwalk Connecticut

Success Checklist from The Wizard of Oz

Here are some of the things I've done throughout my career to help keep me on track. I learned a lot of them from Dorothy.

Does Dorothy use a checklist to help her reach her goal? Probably not.

But since she seems to be doing all the right things, it makes me wonder.

So, in order to help you make your way down your own Yellow Brick Road, I've devised a checklist of the essential lessons I've learned from Dorothy and *The Wizard of Oz* about achieving goals. I've had a great laboratory to experiment in: I call it my life.

I perfected the use of the following items during the course of my career. These are strategies that definitely helped me achieve a high level of success.

Wizard Wisdom: *A checklist is one of the best tools you'll ever use in achieving your dreams. Don't underestimate its value!*

The ideas on the Success Checklist came from observing Dorothy and the situations she finds herself in. In *The Wonderful Wizard in You!* you'll see how Dorothy's incredible story perfectly parallels your own life. I believe—no, scratch that, I *know*—that these things are essential for everyone trying to achieve whatever it is that they personally define as Success.

The Wizard in You Success Checklist

Learn to Believe in Yourself
Develop a Perfect Clear Image of Your Goal
Begin Moving Forward

37

Be with People Who Believe in You and Support You
Learn to Respond, Not React
Get Yourself a Mentor
Commit Your Plan to Paper
Develop Self-Discipline
Avoid Avoidance
Improve Your Talent for Solving Problems
Continuously Refine Your Plan
Become an Expert at Patience and Perseverance
Ceaselessly Move Forward—and Never, Ever Let Up!

Learn to Believe in Yourself

Believe in yourself—even when the deck is stacked
against you. Make sure you learn to believe in yourself.
It is an important skill, and it can be learned. Nothing—and I
mean nothing—is more powerful than a genuine belief in yourself.

Want a perfect example of a terrific person who, no matter what, just wouldn't give up?

OK.

Jackie Robinson, the first black baseball player to play in the major leagues, was a born warrior.

Jackie Robinson was conceived, born, and raised while chaos raged around him and his family. That chaos was fed by segregation, racism, and a total deprivation of those rights that white Americans took for granted.

During his early adult life, Jackie volunteered to fight for a nation that sought to deny him the right even to take the seat of his choice on a bus. His conviction and strength of character and desire to be treated as an equal and as a human being, even in the face of a military court-martial, serve as hallmarks to his legacy.

Although that "war" still raged even when he was selected to play for the Brooklyn Dodgers AAA farm team, his indomitable spirit, coupled with his phenomenal athletic ability, carried him through. Spiked by opposing players, ducking "errant" pitches, and ignoring racial epithets, he brought "America's game" to a new level without sinking to a lower one. If only the rest of America would follow suit nowadays.

"Lions, tigers, and bears, oh my!" Well, what of "lairs, Klansmen, and lynchings, oh my"?

For Dorothy, it is the fear of what may be hidden in the shadows that presents the greatest obstacles to overcome.

For Jackie, it was the fear of what he knew was hiding in the shadows that spurred him on.

Kind of puts the everyday obstacles that we overcome in our business and personal worlds into perspective, doesn't it?

Great Scene #3

Dorothy is told, no matter what happens, "Just follow the Yellow Brick Road." Once Dorothy knows where it is she wants to go, Glinda prods along her by saying, "It's always best to start at the beginning."

There's a significant scene in the film when the Wicked Witch cackles, whirls around, and vanishes in a burst of smoke and fire and a clap of thunder.
That is a terrifying moment for Dorothy—and for most people who see the movie.
Anyway, after Dorothy is threatened, Glinda tells her she's made a very bad enemy in the form of the Wicked Witch of the West, and the sooner she gets out of Oz, the better.
Dorothy says she'd give anything to get out of Oz and back home but doesn't know how. Glinda advises her to go to Emerald City to consult the Wizard of Oz himself. Dorothy wonders how she can get there.
Dorothy asks Glinda how to get from Munchkin Land to the Emerald City to see the Wizard.
Glinda tells her that it's always best to start at the beginning and to just follow the Yellow Brick Road.

You would think that answer deserves a "Duh!"
But you'd be surprised to know that most ventures fail because people do *not* begin at the beginning. They go off half-cocked without first establishing a good plan.
In our business and personal lives, we learn that the most effective thing you can do when start any project is to begin with the end in mind.

Let's face it. It's hard to get where you want to—unless you first know where you're going and why you're going there.

Once you find out where you are now, where you want to go, and how you're going to get there, just take Glinda's advice and "Follow the Yellow Brick Road."

Where's the Yellow Brick Road in your life?

Where does it begin? And more importantly, where's it going to take you?

Have you acknowledged that it even exists in your life?

Have you mapped it out?

Do you accept that it's going to be an imperfect road, with obstacles and detours along the way?

Right before Dorothy steps onto the Yellow Brick Road, she turns to the Glinda and, frightened, asks, "What happens if I . . .?"

Glinda cuts her off and says, "Just follow the Yellow Brick Road."

In other words, *get going!*

Then, stay on track.

Don't ever let up and don't ever let go.

Don't stop.

Don't let anybody influence you negatively.

Stay on your course.

And don't even really entertain those doubts that are assuredly going to arise.

Just stay on the Yellow Brick Road. Deal with the obstacles as they present themselves, and most importantly, *learn* from them!

How You Got Where You Are Today

Did you get blown away by some kind of tornado?
Or are you personally responsible for where you are?

To get where you are today did not require any magic, just as Dorothy used common sense and persistence to get back to Kansas.

What I mean when I say "magic" is this: I don't think you had to do anything too spectacular to get to where you are.

Most of us just end up where we are by chance.

We reacted to life, we didn't really plan it.

It's the domino theory.

When you stack up a thousand single dominos, in the right order, the right way, and you push the first one over, all the rest of them go down. Right to the very end. Just the way you wanted them to.

Once you start, if you plan and space them properly, you won't be able to stop the dominoes from doing what you programmed them to do—even if you change your mind.

All this business about finding the way to get things done, making the plan for the road to Success—they aren't five or six giant dominoes, the giant parts of your plan. It's the little, tiny things you do every day that make the plan work.

Of course, you definitely need a plan, a map, a route to travel, but just set it up the right way, do what you've planned to do, press the first one, keep doing the right things, and they will all go down, one after another.

Insight from Oz: I think a successful life is just a continuous sequence of doing the right things. When you have a good plan, the problems everyone encounters are just that—problems—not major catastrophes. They may slow you down or cause a temporary detour, but they don't ruin the entire journey.

Enjoy Your Own Yellow Brick Road—
Both the Good and the Bad

Let's say I'm talking to a prospective buyer whom I offer a chance to buy a vial of a new miracle antibiotic.

Now, if this particular prospect has a 98.6°F temperature and is perfectly healthy, no matter what I charge for this vial, even only five cents, my prospect won't buy it. She doesn't need it, and so she won't pay for it. That makes sense.

Now, let's take another situation.

A prospect has an infection, feels terrible, and has a 104.5°F temperature. The miracle antibiotic is guaranteed to reduce your temperature to normal within three minutes. The prospect knows that if the fever gets much higher, there'll be brain damage. Suddenly $15,000 looks like a cheap price to pay for a couple of ounces of liquid. The prospect will buy. The fever's up.

If you are my prospect, and your fever is the need to succeed, and a normal temperature means you have that need under control and on a program to get you there, then you'll pay. You'll pay whatever it takes to get that fever under control. You'll pay because you'll see a benefit to the expense.

Well, this fever idea works both for you, as someone seeking a map for the road to Success, and it works in selling, where you have to learn to get your own prospects' fevers high enough to motivate them to pay for what you are offering.

Are you 98.6 or are you 104.5?

If you want to be 98.6, that's cool, but you'll be 98.6 forever. You'll be very normal and you'll go along more or less just fine. You'll be ordinary. But I think you want to be extraordinary, don't you? If you are comfortable, if your temperature is 98.6, you'll never buy into it, you'll never buy into the costly plan to get to Success.

I keep talking about how much Success costs.

What do I mean?

I mean that Success is expensive. It takes lots of hours, lots of commitment, lots of sacrifice. Lots of doing things even if you don't feel like it. I know this recovering alcoholic. "Been sober for years and years—fifteen years." Yet, to this very day, every morning he gets up, looks himself in the mirror, and says, "I'm not going to take a drink today, *even if I feel like it!*"

Is there anything you can promise yourself you won't do today, even if you really feel like it? Do you tend to procrastinate? Do the easy things instead of the difficult ones? Avoid making sales calls?

> **Insight from Oz:** *There's an old saying, "Pleasant methods—or pleasant results." Take your choice. You can either work hard now for great rewards later, or you can take it easy now and get what you deserve later.*

Sometimes you have to get your own fever way up there on purpose, to psyche yourself up.

Well, I'm at 104.5 degrees most of my life. I'm always buying vials of miracle drugs—that is, I'm always prepared to pay the price. I'm always willing to do what it takes in order to succeed.

Now, are you going to fix it or not? Are you going to fix this problem? It's up to you. As you go through life, things are going to pop up—like it or not.

You're going to be offered a miracle drug. At one point in time your fever will get to 104.5. You have to pay for it then. You'll have to have the $15,000. You'll have to have the sense of purpose, the dream, the goal, the discipline, and the motivation.

Know Your Comfort Level

It is necessary to try to surpass one's self always;
this occupation ought to last as long as life.

—Queen Christian of Sweden

Here's a story that demonstrates the importance of knowing what you are comfortable with—and what you are not comfortable with.

Chuck was a man who used to work for me. He came from Grainfield, Connecticut, and he came at a time when I needed somebody to handle the back-end service of my client relationships, and he came like a house on fire, ready to take on the world. At least that's what he told me.

Some people can get five years' experience during five years— and others can get one years' experience five times in that same period. They don't grow as fast as they could or should grow.

Now, "could" and "should" are my words, not Chuck's words.

Chuck thought he was growing. Chuck thought he was improving in what he used to do because he could now do it better. But the fact of the matter is, doing what you used to do a little bit better is not growing.

If you only do what you've been doing, you only get what you've been getting. If you do it a little better, you'll get a little more.

And the fact is that all he got was what he was getting.

During his final twelve months here, all we were doing was fighting with each other.

Why?

Because I wasn't getting something new, something refreshing, something different, something enthusiastic. It just wasn't ever coming.

So it became clear that I was probably going to have to go to Chuck and say something like, "Chuck, either you have to begin growing—growing significantly, geometrically, in your education, experience, training, and attitudes—or else I'm going to have to get somebody else who will."

He must have felt that because he decided he couldn't or wouldn't change, he'd leave the situation. He must have figured he couldn't take the pressure, which is the old story about if you can't stand the heat, get out of the kitchen.

Well, he got out of the kitchen, and we replaced him with somebody who likes being in the kitchen, somebody who wants to grow and who likes to grow.

This is all about the whole thing we talked about before, about finding out what you want—and getting out there and starting to do it. Chuck didn't want any more tomorrow than he had today.

Don't think I don't like Chuck, because that is simply not true. He was and is very happy and he got what he wants, and that's the name of the game here.

Chuck got what he wanted. He got to come in at 9 P.M., go home at 5 P.M., and relax on Saturday and Sunday. That's all he wanted, and he was willing to accept the reward of that kind of situation, whatever it might be. He earns a basic salary, drives a basic car, lives in a basic home, and has a completely satisfactory basic lifestyle. He's happy with that.

Now, if that's what he wants, more power to him, because he bought and paid for what he wants and he seems to be happy. He's not saying, "Gee, I'd like to have more, but I don't want to pay for it and so now I'm unhappy."

Instead, he says, "I'm getting what I work for, and I'm comfortable with knowing I'm getting it fair and square."

Patrick, the guy I had working for me in that position before Chuck, is now back with me. Patrick wants the world and is willing to pay for it with effort. He's always willing to come in here at 7 in the morning and go home 7 or 8 at night. I did it myself back then, and I'm still doing it now.

These two good men represent two completely different personalities. Both seem to be happy, both seem to be getting what they want, and both are on a journey that is comfortable for them. I think it's a very important story to think about. The point of it is to make up your mind, and whichever way you choose to go, go at it with gusto.

Now, as for Chuck, I think he thought five years ago that because he was working so hard for me then that he could do it on his own. He thought it would be very simple to go out and sell and do what I do. "All you have to do is work hard and people will buy," he thought.

Chuck forgot that there's another piece besides working hard—you have to sell hard, too. In my insurance business, you get paid really well for finding people who are interested in buying.

You don't get paid for selling to them because just by finding someone interested in buying, you've already done the hard part. People pay you for doing the hard part, not the easy part.

Once you've identified a good prospect, the selling is the easy part. The whole business of selling is not selling, as people think. The whole business of selling is *finding* them.

Chuck couldn't find them.

He paid a price for working hard in the back room. He found a niche that he was good in—doing the back-end work, supporting me in making sales, and servicing clients from his office in the back room.

He decided he wanted to go to the front room. He thought he'd find happiness there.

Then he went out and his whole job became not the daily routine support activities he was so good at, but the difficult business of finding new prospects. That's the hardest part, and he found he couldn't do that as well as what he did in his back-room niche.

It took him five years out in the world running his own business to learn that lesson and he was unhappy that whole time. He was trying to do something he was not equipped to do.

He's not a prospector.

He was not a find-'em guy, so all the time he was doing it his stomach was tied up in knots every single day. Another day, another knot. He was doing something he hated.

Once Chuck learned what it means to do something he loves, he's come back to doing it and now he's in perfect shape again. The knots went away. He doesn't visit a psychiatrist anymore. He has a different perspective. He's on a different track now.

It is true that he may not make as much money as he would have if he could have overcome those knots and had no problem prospecting. But at least he's happier in this new arrangement, and he's making more money than he ever thought he could make by doing what he really likes to do. He's comfortable.

And that's what we were talking about earlier.

Take Action for Success!: *Do what you like. Develop a system that eliminates all the things you don't like to do. Put a system in effect that guarantees that those things will get done by someone else if not you, and then fill your day with the things you do like. It's not some pipe dream. Anybody who tries really can make it work for them. It's all in how carefully and thoughtfully you design your system.*

My new guy's now developing a new way to do the old job—so he can grow. He's not satisfied with just doing the old job a little bit better. He wants to find a way to take it to the next level.

When he came back, he said, "Sidney, I want the back room again—but how can I make more money than just a back-room guy?"

So *he* gave *me* some new chores. I hire him, but he puts me to work to help him find ways to make more money! You have to like that spirit!

So now, I like it and he likes it. He's doing what he likes. He's giving me what I need and want, and now it's a good relationship again, something the other guy would never have given me.

He couldn't have.

He didn't want what I wanted.

I'd ask Chuck for more and more. Put more and more pressure on him, demand more and more from him, and then he'd say "Hold it! No more! Enough already!"

This new guy's coming up to me all the time, bugging me, saying, "Sid, anything else you want me to do?" He's making more work for himself. "What else can I give you so I can make more money?"

The two people—both getting what they want—are now getting their own way. Both are wonderful people, perfect people. I wouldn't have fired Chuck. I would have had a difficult time firing him. I would have had to give him six months' notice if I fired him because he was a nice guy. He just couldn't give me what I want because he didn't want it too.

The new guy's giving me what I want because he wants it too, so now I have a whole new territory of productivity. He supports me, makes me more effective, more profitable, more able to serve my clients, more able to find new ones.

Whatever I ask him to do, he says, "Good, Sid, I'll do that."

There are no limits. That's kind of the way it is.

Everybody doesn't have to drive the bus. Some people can sit and relax.

A car has four or five seats and only one steering wheel, so some people sit and relax while the driver takes them wherever they are going.

Other people want to be the driver. As long as you know which one you are, it's easy. But a lot of friction and discomfort comes from not having sat down and thought it out, in not having figured out what you want to do.

You see, you can't sit in the back and drive—that would leave you feeling pretty frustrated. But, if you decide to, you can sit in the front and relax. You have to know where you want to be. As long as you know that, I think you have a great chance to hit a home run.

Who Needs a Mentor?

"It's nice work if you can get it, and you can get it if you try!"

That song lyric reminds me of the value of finding a mentor.

Mentors are great. They can save you hundreds of years of trial and error when they share their experience with you. And, if they are inclined, they can open many doors for you.

But the most amazing thing about the universe of mentors is how relatively easy they are to find—and engage.

A mentor is a good thing if you can get one, and you can get one if you try!

Wizard Wisdom: *Find a mentor. Learn from those people around you—even if it turns out to be a little dog. Look at successful people, emulate what they do, and then do it as well.*

A mentor could be your priest or your rabbi. A mentor can be a man or a woman, young or old, black or white. He could be your boss, or she could be your neighbor. She may be an expert in your chosen field, or he can be someone who has no direct experience in what you want to do or be, but he may have lots of business or people sense.

He may take you under his wing and help you.

The people that do get to be successful have certain key ingredients. One of the ingredients they all seem to have is a high need to succor. The mentor may make $2.6 million a year, and you may make only 25 grand. It doesn't matter. Most successful people have a high need to help people, and you just may be the one whom that successful person is willing—or needs—to help.

List a dozen potential mentors, people who you would like to meet in your field or in your community. I'm not talking about going to the president of the United States. I'm talking about somebody in your community, somebody whom you know—or know of— somebody who lives in an affluent neighborhood. Somebody who owns a major business. Somebody who is successful—however you define success. Go after that person. Think how flattering it might be if you were to call that potential mentor on the phone and say "Hi, my name is Joe Smith, and I'm a person who doesn't own very much, but I have a lot of dreams and hopes. I'm doing research on becoming successful myself, and I wonder if I could spend a half hour with you to find out how you got to be so successful?"

I really find it very difficult to think that somebody would not accept that challenge, that opportunity to help. If they have any kind of heart at all, they're going to want to help you. Maybe they will legitimately be too busy, or maybe they are already helping lots of other people. And maybe they'll refer you someone else they know, perhaps someone else in their organization.

Who knows? It might turn out to be a great way to meet someone and get a job, or it might be an opportunity for that person to say, "You're the kind of person I want in my company. I want to spend more time with you."

I don't know exactly how it you would work it, but it would be a start. As an employer of more than two hundred people, I can guarantee you that when I meet someone who I think is competent, on the ball, and can do a good job, I'm interested. I'm really interested! Good people are hard to find and harder to keep. As you'll read later on in this book, when it comes to finding a good secretary, I heartily recommend that you skip hiring one—and go directly to stealing one. Good secretaries are worth their weight in gold, and training one takes way too much time—too much downtime. But when you come across a good secretary and make an offer that can't be refused, you're ahead of the game.

Insight from Oz: When it comes to finding and taking advantage of a mentor, don't hesitate to be aggressive. When someone is aggressive in trying to get through to me, when someone finds a way to sneak past my secretary, I pay attention to that person. I know I'm dealing with someone who has a high level of energy, someone who is hell-bent on succeeding.

Wizard Wisdom: There's nothing wrong with building a castle in the sky. Just make sure you get good and busy building real foundations under it.

Other Ways to Get the Wisdom Mentors Offer

People often underestimate the value of books and tapes, but it's a mistake to pass them up.

Why? I'll tell you why: because books and tapes represent the very best thinking that successful people have to offer. And their thinking isn't glib, off-the-top-of-their-heads noise. The material that winds up in their books has been carefully planned, organized, presented, and edited.

Now, I know there are only so many hours in the day available for you to study success ideas, so it's your responsibility to carefully select the material you will study.

The library is full of books, videotapes, and audiotapes about how successful people, business leaders, politicians, actors, artists, and others made it to the top. Robert Townsend, ex-chairman of a major car-rental company, has a book and audiotape called *Up the Organization*. It's great to listen to. He's fabulous. You listen to that tape and you get a whole new take on what it takes to be successful in any organization.

Another great example is Harvey Firestone, telling how he built the Firestone Tire Company. There are hundreds of successful people who have produced books and tapes in which they tell you the specifics of how they excelled in their fields.

> **Insight from Oz:** *Ask people you respect (or successful people you know) to recommend the books and tapes that have helped them. You'll be surprised at how often you'll get a helpful response.*

Norman Schwartzkopf is a great example of a mentor, and how he led the war is a great story. The guy wasn't great for a long time as far as the public knew. But he was great for decades—it's just that nobody knew how great. His is an interesting story.

Norman was a big-time general, in the service for thirty or more years. And until recently, after all those years in the service, he was making just $110,000 a year. And he worked around the clock, seven days a week. And he was a pretty successful guy, it seems, or else they wouldn't have put him in charge. As it turned out, the reason he was in charge of that war was because he spent most of his life there in the Middle East. He knew the culture and the customs.

Once he began managing that operation, he spearheaded the allied victory, and he did it in just ninety-one hours. Of course, the publicists stretched it to one hundred hours for appearances' sake. So guess what? He suddenly got an advance of $5 million on his book. Now he's making $60,000 a speech, and he's doing it three times a week. Now he's making more in two days a week than he was making in a whole year.

So, although he'd been successful all his life, what happened is that they unwrapped the box, and the real Norman came out.

If I had asked Norman one year before he was involved in that war, "Hey Norm, are you going to be making $180,000 a week anytime soon, or writing a book and getting an advance of $5 million?" he'd have said, "Sid, get out of the room. You're crazy!"

Why wouldn't he have believed it?

Easy. Because he didn't have that dream. But apparently, sometime during that war, he saw he was going to succeed. He got a glimpse of how valuable he could be on the bookstore shelves and on the lecture circuit. Now he's making a lot of money.

He now has a whole new career that he never had before, one that he probably envisioned.

What is there about you that you need to get a glimpse of? If you are an ordinary person who can get a glimpse of your own unique talents and skills, you can get a glimpse of what that dream could look like if it were to become a reality.

And then you can go about making it into a reality.

Great Scene #4

Toto discovers a talking scarecrow who thinks he hasn't any brains, but he's smart enough to try to do something about it. Negative thinking permits us to believe inaccurate and damaging things about ourselves.

It is Toto, presumably a dumb dog, who shows Dorothy that the Scarecrow can talk.

This is significant because it shows that often the people we perceive as being able to see less are often able to see more—or at least differently—than we do.

Dorothy's immediate response to seeing the Scarecrow in the cornfield is that he is "just another scarecrow," no different from the hundreds she'd seen in Kansas. Imagine thinking this in such a decidedly magical place, where nothing is as it actually seems.

It takes her dog Toto, a presumably "lesser being," to alert her to the fact that this scarecrow is very different from any she had encountered in Kansas.

Their meeting each other at the crossroads is an important event.

Dorothy is faced with making a decision: Go it alone or allow the Scarecrow to accompany her.

The Scarecrow asks where she is going and she tells him. When she tells him, he asks if she thinks the Wizard might be able to provide him with some brains. She tells him that even if he didn't, he'd be no worse off than he is now.

Dorothy has a momentary second thought, warning the Scarecrow that she's got a witch mad at her, and that fact might put him in jeopardy.

But the Scarecrow says there's nothing he's afraid of—
with the exception of a lighted match.

The Scarecrow tells Dorothy that he'd face a "whole
box full" of angry witches for the chance of getting a
brain. And a moment later, Dorothy agrees.

They both shout "To Oz!" link arms, and go marching
down the Yellow Brick Road.

The Scarecrow thought that if perhaps he joined Dorothy, the
Wizard might give him a brain. But what if he wouldn't?

Dorothy replies "Well, perhaps, but you wouldn't be any worse off
than you are now."

Right.

So, what is the point here?

Answer: *You've got to take the chance.*

Extraordinary vs. Ordinary People

I know this isn't that obvious to most people, but it sure is obvious to me: Everything that goes on, all the extraordinary things you
hear and read about, *are all done by ordinary, everyday people!*

Dorothy and her pals are extraordinary all along—they just need
something to happen to help them recognize it.

Extraordinary things are accomplished by ordinary people!

How can that be?

No matter what research I see, no matter what studies I look at, it
all shakes out about the same: Everybody is born with the same relative amount of skin, blood, hair, brains, and ability to work hard.
Sure, there are legitimate differences—a few IQ points here, a few
inches of height there.

Still, despite the fact that everyone has the same amount of stuff
to start off with, they all wind up so differently. What's going on?

People—whether they're astronauts, brain surgeons, or truck
drivers—all start out the same way. And what makes one person go
one way and another go the other way is still a mystery.

But the fact is, they are all ordinary people who began doing
extraordinary things by the way they went about their business.

If we cut open the brain surgeon's skull alongside a truck driver's,
we might find that their brainpower is probably within 1 percent of

each other. If one uses 25 percent of his brain, the other may use 26 percent.

Why is it that between two people with exactly the same brain-power, one is driving a truck for $27,000 a year (and there's nothing wrong with driving a truck by the way; I'm just demonstrating the differences in earning power) and the other is performing brain surgery for $1,027,000 a year. What's the difference?

I don't think it has to do with your physical attributes. It has to do with what you want to do with what you have. It does help to have had a great environment, upbringing, personal relationships, and good people in your life. But you may have had lived in a terrible environment, had a rotten upbringing, lousy relationships, and met only low-life good-for-nothings. If that's the case, and if you can recognize it and move beyond it and work a plan that leads you in the general direction of Success, you are bound to come out a winner.

And another thing: Where you are today has a lot to do with people who told you in your early years that you could or couldn't succeed.

If you have negative tapes playing in your head, think about them carefully so that you are aware of how they have brainwashed you, and then work hard to negate them. Eliminate them. You can't go back and fix the yesterdays; you can't change them. But you can start with today and all the tomorrows. You can evaluate where you are today, how you got here and what you heard, and make required changes.

"Be yourself!" is just about the worst advice you can give some people.

—Anonymous

Insight from Oz: In times of stress, conflict, pressure, and change, those negative tapes often kick in as the automatic response and reaction to such situations. Awareness is the key to identifying and eliminating automatic negative reactions. And importantly, don't allow the void you create by getting rid of those automatic reactions to be filled back up with more negatives. Make a conscious effort to plug positive "can do!" programs into the empty spaces.

Learn to Respond, Not React

Don't be a hapless victim when opportunity
knocks or when things go wrong. Be a fighter.

Wizard Wisdom: *Successful people consistently do what others can do but won't.*

Don't react to things as they happen.

Respond to them. There's a big difference.

In one scenario, let's say you're sitting somewhere, minding your own business, and someone suddenly comes up and takes a swing at you. You flinch and duck out of the way. That's your *reaction.*

See why this one belongs on our checklist?

In another scenario, let's say that instead of flinching, you just reach up with your left forearm to deflect the punch and lunge with your right fist upward to thump your assailant.

That's a *response.*

Which is more productive?

Wizard Wisdom: *A dream doesn't come any closer by itself. You have to run after it.*

Not Everyone Gets to Oz—Some Folks Just Give Up

I once saw a stand-up comedian doing a show from Las Vegas.

He was complaining about what a loser he is. How nothing he does ever works out. How every bet he makes, he loses. Then he said something that struck me funny. He said that if some guy would

57

follow him around and do the *exact opposite* of everything he did, that guy would be a multimillionaire in no time.

So that made me start thinking about the qualities of people who are not successful. I describe them here so that you can recognize them and do just the opposite.

Most people are just ordinary. They just go along their whole lives in a very regular, unexceptional way. I guess they accomplish more or less what they want to accomplish, but they always yearn for something more—and they rarely get it.

Why?

Well, for one thing, they don't seem to go over the top of the mountain for themselves. They can't get over. They get to where they're going, but without any real zest or any real accomplishment, and when they put their head on the pillow at night they say, "Jeez, I know I'm capable of so much more!" Then they just fall asleep wondering, "How come I'm not getting there?"

Let me describe some of the things that people who are ordinary do. These ideas describe why they don't experience tremendous success, and maybe even why they fail.

Nothing is so difficult as not deceiving oneself.

—Ludwig Wittgenstein

Self-Preoccupation Is an Expensive Luxury

Self-absorbed people are hypnotically interested in themselves. And other people find that boring. Self-absorbed people are primarily concerned with themselves and what's on their minds.

They haven't got enough time to think about anybody else because they're so concerned with what they're doing or not doing that they haven't got time to think about the next person and what the next person needs. And that applies to the next priority, the next important step, the next thing coming down the road that really deserves 1000 percent of their attention and concentration.

Their arrows all point in. There are no arrows pointing out. And, probably because of their way of relating and reacting to the world, they . . .

Can't Handle Responsibility

Remember how frightened the Scarecrow seems when Dorothy first meets him? He refuses to even try to think of any solutions because he doesn't *believe* he can. He simply refuses to take any responsibility for his situation. That nearly costs him his life.

When they eventually do find themselves responsible for something—in business, for example—they are full of enthusiasm and say, "I'll take on this job and do a bang-up job like you've never seen!" But a funny thing happens. The sum total of their interest and enthusiasm is used up in making that statement! They've got nothing left to carry out their promise.

So what happens is that other people come not to rely upon them. And because of that, they don't get the job again and begin feeling less than capable. They could've had the whole thing work out differently if they would have taken the job and dealt with the initial challenges that scared them off. They are capable of taking the job and assuming the responsibility and making it happen—they just don't do it.

They also suffer from a . . .

Lack of Empathy

Empathy simply means being able to put yourself in the other person's shoes. And several times when Dorothy can use an assist, the Cowardly Lion is too concerned about his own personal safety to think of his friends.

These people—they can't do that. Probably for the same reason they are self-preoccupied. Until they can put themselves in your shoes, they can't think about how you feel, and if they can't think about how you feel, then they can't know what you want or need, and they can't do what you would do. They can function in one narrow little job—and I am not saying there is anything wrong with that, but that kind of approach to life is not one of the essential ingredients of success. In a nutshell, those who are not natural empathizers and those who will not make the effort to learn how to be empathetic are just not highly effective people.

Closed-Mindedness

Closed-minded people, as I see it, are people who are afraid of change.

At first, the Tin Man, the Scarecrow and the Lion all thought they couldn't overcome their perceived problems. In the end, they were proven wrong about their flaws. But in life, many people never give themselves the chance to find out. They give up way too soon. Giving up is like agreeing to die earlier than you have to.

People who suffer from closed-mindedness do not permit anything to enter their minds—at least in terms of ideas. Oh, sure, they'll watch a new TV show or try a new topping on a pizza—maybe. But any ideas that don't conform to their existing views of the world—forget it. They're so busy doing what they've been doing that they can't get to a clear place to launch a new plan.

As I have said earlier, if you only do what you've been doing, you'll only get what you've been getting.

People with closed minds won't grow, and they can't convince themselves to do anything other than what they have been doing. And if they can't convince themselves, they certainly . . .

Can't Persuade Others

Unsuccessful salespeople, those who haven't yet found their Wizard, usually have difficulty persuading others to do what has to be done. The root of this problem is the lack of empathy and closed-mindedness.

Because of their lack of empathy, they can't really understand how the other person feels and therefore can't offer any solutions to the problems other people face. And because their minds are closed, they can't change to accommodate sales prospects and their needs.

People don't rush to work with this kind of person because they seem to be . . .

Naive in Business

Ordinary people don't understand that business is transaction.

You give and you get. That's a pretty simple definition of business. All the rest is detail. In order to succeed, people need to have a clear understanding of what they must give in return for what they will ultimately get.

And when they don't understand what it takes to become successful in business, they figure their best bet is to only do as little as they can.

"If I can goof off three out of eight hours a day and still get my paycheck, isn't that really smart!" they think. They may think they've satisfactorily done their jobs, but if they ever stop to analyze it (fat chance!), they will realize they've succeeded—at doing as little as they can. They can't even see what a better situation would be like because of another problem, which is that they are . . .

Unimaginative

All this type of people sees is what they want to see.

They can't see past what's right in front of them. And they can't see down the road six days, let alone six weeks, six months, or six years. They're so busy in what they're doing that they can't think about what else has to be done or what the bigger picture is. They don't see the tremendous potential in all that the forest has to offer because they have their noses pressed up against the bark of the one single tree they are working on.

Even if they wanted to, they couldn't crane their necks to look around the tree because they are so . . .

Inflexible

They will not make any changes in their lives. They will not be accommodating, and they will not do anything for anybody that does not absolutely, definitely have to be done.

It's an "It ain't my job" way of seeing things. "I mean, I've done all I can. It's not my job to do it," they whine.

These people are good at putting themselves in a box and keeping themselves there.

They can't perceive the total picture. All they see is where they are and they can't see past their nose, so all they do is what they think they have to do and therefore, they never grow.

Resent Authority

"You're going to tell me what to do?" they say, barely masking their anger. "I know what has to be done. It's my job!"

Even if the person in authority is making a good point about something, people who resent authority react negatively. Authority threatens them because is raises the possibility of change. And ordinary people naturally are conservative. They want to conserve the situation just as it is.

"Leave it alone. If it ain't broke, don't fix it." Anyone who knows me knows that my motto is: "If it ain't broke, break it—then make it better!"

When you look at the whole package of personality traits of ordinary people, you see how all of these qualities seem to go together, especially . . .

Laziness

They don't want to do what has to be done in the morning to get the priorities out of the way, to clear their desks for the new things that they know full well will be coming at them all day long. They make a list and sometimes do what the list says, but usually not. For the most part, they don't really get active and get down to doing what has to be done—except when it comes time to be . . .

Critical and Blaming

"It wasn't my fault."

"Somebody pulled *my* tail!"

"I didn't do it."

"I mean, they told me to do this and I did what I was told."

Yeah, sure.

At no point are they even thinking about creating or about making things better. Just go through the motions and it'll probably work out. And if it doesn't, so what? Who cares?

Insight from Oz: If you are reading this book, you are one of the people who are asking themselves, "How come I'm not getting where I want to be?" It's a good question to ask yourself, and by paying attention to how ordinary people conduct themselves, you'll have good examples—not to follow!

Great Scene #5

A Cowardly Lion tries—and fails—to intimidate Dorothy and her crew. The Lion reverts to behavior he's familiar with in times of stress, even though what he does is ineffective. People do that all the time.

While Dorothy, the Scarecrow, and the Tin Man proceed down the Yellow Brick Road, singing and worrying about lions and tigers and bears (oh my!), they just about jump out of their shoes at the sound of a deep roar nearby.

From out of nowhere, a lion appears.

And he's behaving menacingly. He teases and taunts the Tin Man, Dorothy, and the Scarecrow. He roars menacingly. He calls Scarecrow a "lopsided bag of hay" and the Tin Man a "shivering junkyard."

At this moment, Toto begins to bark at the lion. (Toto again!)

You know, I believe Toto's the most underrated character in *The Wizard of Oz*!—and here's more evidence to support that.

He's the one who seems to be there every time something significant takes place.

In this scene, the Lion growls at Toto, as if about to attack. Dorothy screams at the Lion, but Toto just jumps into the fray. He chases after the Lion, and then the Lion chases Toto. Toto's action causes Dorothy to intervene; she picks up Toto and slaps the Lion across his nose.

Suddenly, the Lion starts to cry like a baby.

Did you catch that?

The Lion reverts to the familiar—in this case, his *behavior*—during a stressful moment. His behavior (growling and talking tough and bullying creatures smaller than he) probably has not been particularly effective for him.

Yet, even though he's seen the technique fail him—which I'm sure it has, because he's convinced he has no courage—it's the first thing he tries with Dorothy and the crew.

Why? Because even though it doesn't work, it is at least familiar and comfortable. *Just because something is familiar, that doesn't make it right.* That's one thing we can learn about ourselves from the Lion.

Now, the Lion is crying. He's truly hurt that Dorothy has slapped him. He protests that he hasn't hurt Toto, then asks if his nose is bleeding.

After assuring him that he's not bleeding, Dorothy chastises him for picking on someone as small as Toto. She accuses him of being a great big coward.

The Lion begins nervously toying with his tail. He is ashamed of himself. He admits being a courageless coward and says he even scares himself. He's so scared of everything that he hasn't slept in weeks, he says.

The Scarecrow wonders aloud if the Wizard can help the Lion by giving him some courage. Dorothy agrees it's not a bad idea. . . .

One way to keep reminding ourselves about our dreams is to share them with others.

Not only do we have to dream, but we also have to constantly recall them and reinforce them. We have to learn to dream vividly, in sharp, brilliant colors.

Dorothy is always happy to include others on her journey.

Now in this instance, she's a bit off course. She's taking people to see the Wizard, who, as we all know, turns out to be a sham.

But remember, when your motives are positive, the setbacks you experience don't cause as much harm. . . .

Finally, they get ready to return to the Yellow Brick Road. The Lion's still upset and frightened. Dorothy tries to calm him, telling him that the Wizard can solve all their problems.

Wrong, Dorothy! At least not the Wizard you're thinking of, Sweetie.

By this time in the story, I don't think Dorothy has realized that the only "wizard" who can really fix everything is the one who lives inside her, the one who's been with her all along.

No, she hasn't learned that yet lesson yet.

But that makes sense, because her failure to grasp the lesson right away is at the heart of all the action in the tale. Finally coming to understand *and believe* in that lesson is the point of the story and even the book you now hold in your hands.

But Dorothy *is* getting wiser with each step she takes down the Yellow Brick Road.

Unfortunately, the road to wisdom can be counted on to cause a few bumps and bruises for those who travel it. And again, Dorothy demonstrates that she's put all her eggs in one basket (by having total confidence that the Wizard of Oz can fix everything), yet she isn't experienced enough to know whether she's picked the right basket.

Recognize What's Wrong

Analyze the tornadoes in your life.

What are their sources? Did you bring them on yourself? Were you that rare victim of circumstance?

And how are you going to learn from your current tornado in order to be prepared to handle the next one? You can be confident that there will be next ones.

Be honest with yourself—about yourself. There are many people who find it nearly impossible to recognize their own negative traits. Denying them or ignoring them only slows them down.

Most people who fit this profile don't know it.

They have no idea they fall into this category. When they think of negative traits—unless confronted—they almost always think of somebody else's flaws.

They don't know that they're lazy. They don't know that they can't see the whole picture. They don't know that they're unimaginative. They see themselves as very imaginative, but the fact is, the most important thing for them to recognize is what they are blind to. They can't see it when they are lazy and when they are on "stuck."

At best, they're in neutral. Sometimes they're in reverse, but the best they'll be is in neutral.

They're certainly not in drive. If they were, they wouldn't be ordinary.

They'd be extraordinary.

But then why are so few people in the world extraordinary while 99.999 percent are ordinary?

Well, many reasons. Assuming that you can even recognize that you are truly extraordinary—one of the ways that you do so is by looking at what you have accomplished.

Are you getting closer to those dreams that you've talked about all your life?

Are even the ones you don't talk about happening to you?

When you go to sleep at night and you have those wonderful dreams in color, do you make them happen? Do you get what you want most of the time? Do you do what you have promised most of the time?

If you are not getting what you want, if you are not where you want to be, it is essential that you stop, figure out what negative qualities you have (we all have them!), and work on them.

Insight from Oz: There's no magic to any of this. Take a good, long, honest look around—especially in the mirror—and make a list of what you don't like, what is wrong, what you can improve. Then incorporate that list into your overall plan to get to Success. If you do this, I guarantee you'll get there faster!

Winning Traits

What makes a winner?

What makes somebody special?

What makes pros so good at what they do?

How does Dorothy instinctively succeed?

They all have the traits that follow—but with a small twist, maybe just a slight turn of one or two degrees.

Take a look at this list and think about how you may be able to put a twist on some of these things. Think about how you can turn them to your advantage and put your own personal seal on them.

Think about how you can differentiate yourself from everyone else who is trying to do the same thing you are doing.

Most winners have:

A Good Sense of Humor

Winners have a good sense of humor. They take what they *do* very seriously, but they are wise enough not to take *themselves* very seriously,

I say this sometimes when I'm speaking, but my mother says it so wonderfully: "Sonny boy, you see those black hearses that are going by out on the street? They are not practicing."

She's right. They are not practicing. They are for real, and when you're gone, you're gone. And after you've lived a long life and made lots of friends and had a big family, if the weather is rainy and cold, you'll probably have a small turnout at your funeral.

So don't take yourself so seriously!

But do take what you do *very* seriously.

Persistence

Winners won't stop until they get the job done.

Now, these "they" people I'm talking about is who I want you to be.

Don't stop until you finish what you have promised you to do. And don't make the mistake that you can break a promise to yourself. Treat yourself with as much respect as the next person. If it isn't important enough to continue and finish no matter how unpleasant or difficult things get, then don't begin it. There's no point.

If you're going to run in the marathon, I don't care if you win, but if you get in the marathon, finish. No matter what happens. Go the twenty-six miles. If it takes you ten hours or twenty hours, finish.

Balance in Their Lives

A well-balanced diet accommodates all kinds of good things.

The same goes for living a successful life.

Succeeding at one thing does not make a person a success. Keep the "whole person" concept in mind. Think about your business, your family, your children, your hobbies, your charities.

Do they balance? Do they all work in harmony? Do they work in unison? Do they all come together in a healthy way that makes sense for your particular situation?

If not, what specific steps do you need to take in order to put it all into balance?

High Energy

Get up out of bed in the morning at the sound of the alarm clock.

As a matter of fact, why don't do you wake the alarm clock up?

Why don't you get up a few minutes earlier? Train your mind to wake up just a few minutes earlier than everybody else. It's incredible what you can accomplish by waking up just a few minutes earlier, and getting up earlier is a theme that carries itself into all areas of your life.

Their Goals in Mind All the Time

What's the difference between a wish and a goal?

The wish is just a dreamy vague thing floating around out there somewhere.

But a goal! A goal has a deadline. A wish is transformed into a goal when you simply glue a date onto it.

A goal has a date associated with it, and in order to make it happen by that date, you have to do certain things. In order. So you develop a plan to get you from here to there. And each step has certain tasks that need to be done to make your dream come true. And sometimes even those steps have substeps.

But looks what's suddenly happened to your dream!

It's no longer something out there that'll likely never happen.

It's something tangible. It's sitting right there on your desk. Or at least little parts of it are sitting there. Those parts may be in the form of a phone call you have to make, a letter you have to respond to, or a report you have write.

Give your goal a date. Make sure that you do it on the schedule you set for yourself.

As a matter of fact, finish early. Always finish early. By finishing early you'll have more time to do something else—or more time to celebrate having reached your goal. But more importantly, you'll make yourself believe that you're capable of finishing early every single time. You'll teach yourself that all you have to do is apply yourself in order to succeed.

Interest in More Than One Thing

Don't just be focused in one direction.

All work and no play doesn't do anything else for Jack but make Jack some money. And money without a life to go with it is a pretty sad state of affairs.

An Ever-Expanding Base of Knowledge

Keep on learning.

It's been said when you're green, you grow, and when you are ripe, you rot.

You have to stay green.

One of the ways I can suggest you stay green is by teaching. By teaching you'll accomplish much more than you ever could do by learning. So learn your skills, hone them, and then begin teaching others. Teach them for the charities. Teach them for your business. Teach them for your industry. Begin teaching. Begin getting known for doing and practicing what you preach.

Capacity for Empathy

Have some of your arrows pointing outward.

Don't always have them pointing in. Worry about others and how they feel. See if you can put yourself in other people's shoes.

The more you can do that, the more you can appreciate how other people believe and how they feel. Once you do that, the more money you'll make and the more happiness you'll have.

Willingness to Forgive Mistakes

Forgive the ones you make, and forgive the ones others make.

It makes sense to me when I hear people say that nothing good ever happened to them until they began making mistakes.

You will learn more from mistakes than you will from doing things right. Spend time making mistakes. Learn to enjoy them, because if you are working hard and growing and making progress, you'll wind up with lots of scraped knees, egg on your face, and backsliding.

It might be argued that the more mistakes you make, the faster you'll grow—because you'll be learning so much more.

The key is to avoid making those mistakes more than once.

Just make them once, watch out for them again, and get on with it.

Continuous Growth

Find a way to have a high degree of interest in your work.

It's only fair, after all, since that's the way you make your money.

A famous twentieth-century writer's advice to beginning novelists was simply, "Mine deeper!" He didn't want young writers to just describe a cat in the driveway. He wanted them to think about that cat—and what was it doing out there in the driveway, and what might it be thinking about, and whose driveway was it, and what if they came tearing into the driveway nearly running over their cat.

What are the other things about your business that could benefit you if you mined deeper? What other angles are there that you ought to consider? No matter what field you are in, I'm sure there are ways for you to understand what you do in a more profound, professional way.

Think about your interest in your work and how you can get more successful at what you do.

If you really love what you do, you'll probably never "work" another day in your life. Love what you do and keep on doing it.

A Healthy Self-Image

Dorothy teaches the whole crew about that. She has natural self-esteem. She likes herself.

Feel good about yourself. Frankly, by doing all of the previous things we've talked about, you won't be able to help but feel good about yourself.

And along the same line, if you think having a positive attitude is just some corny cliché, think again. Having a positive attitude (which, by the way, is something virtually anyone can develop no matter how bad off they are when they begin) is an absolute necessity in success. It can fuel you during your weak days and spur you to greater heights on your great days.

Insight from Oz: *Now, the synergy of all these items (each by themselves is only one small point) all together will be an absolute explosive event in your life. As you go through every day, every hour of your week, and you keep doing things ordinary people do, you'll succeed—in getting ordinary results. But by being extraordinary, you'll go right through the roof.*

 # Great Scene #6

The Wicked Witch blocks Dorothy's progress just at the brink of her success, but Glinda steps in to help. Even when it seems like victory is within reach, bad things can happen. But if you are on the right road and if you persevere, things will work out.

The Wicked Witch uses the sedative effect of a field of poppies to try to keep Dorothy and her crew from getting to the Emerald City. They fall unconscious in the field. But Glinda had been observing, too, and she sends an invigorating snow shower to rouse them.

The Wicked Witch is in her tower room, peering into the crystal ball. She sees the crew awakening. Cursing Dorothy's good luck, she's suspicious that somebody's always helping her.

What's the point of that?

Well, I think it demonstrates that there are those people in life who are always envious, always jealous, always plotting. But the best defense against them is a good offense. And the elements of a good offense are: know what you want, make a plan to get it, and stick to that plan.

And never, ever, let up!

By the way, the Witch is no slouch either when it comes to persistence.

She takes hold of her broomstick and heads, laughing, for the open window. The Witch has no intention of letting Dorothy enjoy her success in reaching the Emerald City.

The Witch intends to continue plaguing Dorothy.

The Witch plans on making plenty of trouble for Dorothy and her crew, just as the universe had no intention of letting me sit back and relax in Philadelphia.

The situation there, I learned as soon as I arrived, was bad. I had inherited a staff of twenty-one salesmen who couldn't have cared less about insurance.

They all had other jobs—car sales, home improvements, part-time real-estate sales—and they had become accustomed to using the Phoenix office as a coffee shop rather than as the headquarters of their careers.

There was going to be a lot of work for me in Philadelphia, even before I could begin to concentrate on my own personal sales production, which is challenging enough in and of itself.

But I wanted a lot out of life, and I knew I was going to have to put a lot in to get a lot out.

What about you?

How many situations can you look back on in your own life where you came out the loser?

There must have been situations where the challenge was just too much for you to overcome.

When I give 110 percent, lot's of good things happen:

I put myself into a positive frame of mind. I can see clearly what success looks like, and that gives me something to shoot for.

I begin to analyze the problem objectively, without the emotion and fear one normally brings to a tough situation.

And I give myself an action plan.

A Trade Secret

Trade secrets are things I've developed over the years that have given me the edge. They have given me just a few percentage points of an advantage over the competition, and those few percentage points have made all the difference in the world.

Remember, in a race, the difference between first and second place may be nothing more than one-tenth of a second. Slight advantages really do make a difference over time.

The first trade secret I'd like to tell you about is this: Find out what the whole world's doing—and then don't do that.

If you're having to do something expensive, such as buying a $1,500 suit or driving a Rolls-Royce, or if it's something inexpensive, like having a ringing business card or sending outrageous birthday cards, it doesn't matter.

Getting the attention of clients and prospects is what matters.

Even if it's just for the sake of being different, it's worth it.

You have to be able to differentiate yourself from the crowd.

We get this chance to live on this earth. While you're here you should be able to create an image of yourself that makes you different—and better—than your competition so that people remember you for who you are and what you do.

The Only Two Things Worth Worrying About

There are only two things in life worth worrying about.

Number One is *don't sweat the small things.*

Now that is an important rule to keep in mind, but Number Two is even more important than Number One.

Number Two is *they are ALL small things!*

Don't focus on how important you are (because in the grand scheme of things, you're not too important). Instead, try to focus on how important what you do is (because the sum total of what you and everyone else does equals the accomplishments of the entire human race—now, *that's* something that's important). Think about how you can do what you do better today, and tomorrow, and the next day.

Be better at what you do than you were yesterday.

Be better tomorrow than you were today.

Keep on getting better.

Insight from Oz: Improvement comes only from the difficult discipline of striving to meet your goals on a daily, weekly and hourly basis. Every second that Dorothy was in Oz, she was obsessed with getting back to Kansas.

Four Real People

This is a short, short story about taking responsibility—for your life, for your career, for anything.

There are four people involved in this story, and they are named Everybody, Somebody, Anybody, and Nobody.

Imagine that these four people all represent various components of your own personality.

There was an important job to be done, a really important job: a plan to get you going along the road to Success had to be designed.

Everybody was sure that Somebody would do it.

Anybody could have done it, but Nobody wanted to do it.

As a result, Somebody got angry—because it was Everybody's job.

But Nobody asked Anybody.

In the end, the job was never completed. Never got finished.

Everybody blamed Somebody—but the real story, when it comes right down to it, is that actually Nobody asked nobody.

Words from the Wise
Valuable Insights about the Journey—from Successful People

I really never did consider myself successful, and I think that has been a cornerstone to whatever degree of success I *have* achieved. I am always striving to do better, no matter how well it is going. Being a worrywart has probably been good for me because it always had me striving to get better and make sure everything I was doing was right. I have always been a firm believer of Al Gray's *The Common Denominator of Success* and have carried the little yellow pamphlet he published like a bible for many years. I probably give out more copies of it than anyone other than Al Gray himself.

The fact is, we all have choices to make, and frequently it is a choice between either pleasant results or pleasant methods. I also believe in the power of *intention*. I believe we really can find a way to do the things we really intend to do. We all say we are going to do certain things—more than we can do—but the ones we really intend to do are the ones that really get done.

Definitions are important to me, too. Take *character*. Character is the ability to follow through after the exciting feeling we get from events, speakers, and circumstances wears off. Character, to me, means being able to sustain that feeling.

Laziness I define as the fear of defeat. I don't believe that people are consciously lazy. I just think they fear being defeated in whatever it is they want to try. Facing fear dissolves it, and avoiding it compounds it. You probably know of someone who complains that he doesn't feel like working and that he is tired and lazy—but then goes home and jogs eight miles. He suddenly wasn't so tired and lazy when he wanted to do something, something that he knows he can do well.

"When it comes to mistakes I've made, I don't want to get into that right now—it would hog the whole book!"

Bob Yerusalim, CLU, ChFC
Regional Vice President
John Hancock Mutual Life Insurance Company
Marlton, New Jersey

Dreaming in Color

In the film version of *The Wizard of Oz*, I'm sure you recall the dramatic effect achieved when, once out of Kansas and in Munchkin Land, all photography is suddenly in living color.

To me, that symbolizes the need to learn to dream your dream in Technicolor. You have to know the dream inside and out. It has to be clear and vivid.

You might have gotten to where you are today by some hard work, and it's also possible you got what you wanted by accident.

But if you really want to be successful, there are certain things that you must do to make it happen. The things we're talking about in this chapter are the things that you have to do to go from being ordinary to being extraordinary.

Learning to dream in color is an essential ingredient. By dreaming in color, I mean that you concentrate and focus and envision your dream with such crystal clarity that you can practically reach out and touch it.

Did I ever tell you the story about this teenage kid I knew—Freddy, who lived in my neighborhood and went to school with my daughters—who was so anxious to get his driver's license that he was going out of his mind. He was obsessed with the idea of being able to drive. Maybe it was the freedom that being able to drive represented. I don't know exactly what it was. But Freddy loved to make excuses to ride in a car—anytime, anyplace, with anybody. He would sit next to me sometimes and steer an imaginary steering wheel, turning with all the appropriate motions. He'd step on an imaginary accelerator and stomp down on an imaginary break pedal—all perfectly.

Now, the big day came, his sixteenth birthday, and he went to take his driving test. He got in the car with the state trooper, who said, "OK, start the car."

Well, Freddy had fantasized about driving so much that it was just as he had anticipated. And the kid drove like a pro! He was so good that the trooper was sour-faced because he was convinced that Freddy was an experienced driver. But Freddy had never driven a car an inch before that day.

Now that kid knew how to dream in color!

But those things are not overwhelming pieces of a puzzle or a project—instead, they're tiny bites of a giant whole. If you do them right, you can make whatever you want to happen happen. Little by little.

The difference between a standard dream and a vivid Technicolor dream is this: if you're really dreaming, and that dream is superclear, in full color, when you wake up in the morning, you have the picture as clear in your mind then as you did while you were actually dreaming.

A Technicolor dream is much different than a black and white dream that you have at 3 in the morning and by 3:02 is already gone, and you have no recollection of it in the morning. It went through your mind's eye, and it's a nice dream, but that's all it was. Not strong enough to create an active response the next day.

> *Insight from Oz:* Dreaming in color helps you get a picture of what you want that is so clear that you can convert the dream into a goal. You do something about it.

This is the issue: the dream has to be so clear that it'll leave no doubt in your mind that what you are working so hard to get is what you really want.

And once you've learned how to do this, well, then it becomes easier to do it again, and again, and again, and again, and again!

Make your dreams come true by waking up in the morning and doing what you promised yourself during the night when you were dreaming.

Do it! The basic principles of managing yourself can be summarized in one word: *now.* Do it *now.*

Make big changes all of a sudden. Don't be inhibited to absolutely change everything all at once. Don't be embarrassed or hesitant. It'll be OK if people stop and stare and say, "Wow! What's with him?" You can start turning things around today, right now, if you want.

Don't hesitate to shed yourself of your old chains. Sure, people may react funny, but let them.

Grab that dog and go!

Dorothy knows she has to improve her and Toto's situation. Her first step is to step on it!

Take Action for Success!: *This is really where discipline comes in. To make it happen, you have to take all the ideas about what success is to you, create a Things-to-Do List of just these ideas, and put a date next to each item. Then begin doing it all— but only one item at a time. And don't do Number Two until you've finished Number One; don't start Number Three until you've finished . . .*

You're at the point of time where you have to take that dream and fire it out of that grenade launcher with a loud BOOM that will get everybody's attention. You are changing, and things are going to be different.

Discipline is the firepower, and your Technicolor dream is the target.

Fire away!

Distinguishing between Wishes, Dreams, and Goals— Both in Oz and in Your World

I used to get confused about the difference between wishes and dreams and goals.

They're three different kinds of thinking:

A *wish* is something I'd like to have. Dorothy wanted to find a place where there isn't any trouble, somewhere over the rainbow.

A *dream* is something I'd really, really, really want. Dorothy dreams she wants to meet the Wizard.

And a *goal* is a dream that I put a deadline to. Dorothy's goal is to get back to Kansas—as soon as possible!

These are all important. It's up to you to decide which category your thoughts fit into and then take the appropriate action. You decide, then you do something or you do nothing.

And that's why Dr. Maxwell Maltz wrote his wonderful book *Psycho-Cybernetics*. People would come to Dr. Maltz, a plastic surgeon, and say, "I'd like you to fix my nose."

And he would say, "Why do you want your nose fixed?"

"Well, I'm an ugly duckling, and if I fix my nose, everybody will love me. And if everybody loves me, I'll feel better."

And he'd say, "I tell you what: instead of me fixing your nose, why don't we fix your head? Then I won't have to fix your nose."

And he began fixing people psychologically instead of surgically.

I have read his book more than two hundred times. That's not an exaggeration. *At least two hundred times.* It teaches me something every time I read it.

Dr. Maltz says you can have anything you want as long as you dream clearly enough about what you want, and the dream must be in color.

Take Action for Success!: You must do it, and do it, and do it, he urges people. And you must practice it for twenty-one days without letup. At the end of twenty-one days, it will be burned in your brain.

That's what I'm talking about when I talk about dreaming. Make it a recurrent dream if you want it come true.

There's nothing I ever wanted in my life that I didn't dream about first.

That's how I bought my first Rolls-Royce. I wanted it so much that not only did I dream about it, I went to visit my dream—right in the car dealer's showroom. I did that so I could dream about it in better detail. I actually sat in the car. Through sheer will and hard work, I made that car mine.

Once a month, on Saturday mornings, I went there to the showroom. I touched and felt and smelled the car. I knew I had to wait thirty-one days before I would let myself go back there again. I kept dreaming about how wonderful it would be to own it. To reaffirm my dream, I went back into the showroom, looked at it, and put it back into color again. I smelled and tasted it again. Then I waited another month

And during those thirty-one days, I kept working harder and harder to earn the checks that I need to buy the car. At the end of the thirteenth Saturday visit—thirteen months later—the dream was so clear that it came true.

I drove that Rolls out of there!

The dream became a reality.

And I can think of almost anything I ever wanted—material or emotional—that I literally dreamed into reality. When I go to sleep at night, I put it into my computer in my head, and I dream it and dream it and dream it, and sometimes it happens right away, and sometimes it takes thirteen months, and sometimes it takes even longer. *But it does happen—every single time.*

> **Insight from Oz:** *Maybe I am a natural dreamer. Maybe I'm just built that way, and that's why I've been able to make so many of my dreams come true. But please think about this: I've shared the dream strategy with you. So, even though it didn't occur to you out of thin air, you now know as much about the power of dreaming as I do! So, consider it a gift that I have, but one that I am able to give to you. Please, accept the gift. Do something incredible with it, and then pass it on!*

More Trade Secrets

A Sense of Urgency Is Contagious

When you read or saw *The Wizard of Oz*, I know you must have noticed how dead-on serious Dorothy is about getting back to Oz. Nothing distracts her for long, and the rest of her crew comes to be as focused as she is.

Someone says to me, "Sid, you are a high-energy man. You work a lot of hours; you're generally enthusiastic, generally upbeat. That takes a lot of energy. Where does it come from?"

I believe it's actually up to me. I could be down or I could be up.

Give me one reason, just one, why I should be down.

I can't think of one.

Now, you might say, "Well, not you, Friedman, but me. I can't pay my bills like you can. I don't sell people as well as you. I have problems with my family. I have a disturbed child. My mother's very sick and living in New York. I have lots of problems, so I can't be as up as you can."

Why not?

You're not going to fix the problem being down. Maybe the way to fix the problem is by being up and looking at it in a whole new way. By bringing a sense of urgency to each and every sales situation you enter.

Erase all the negatives that are in your mind right now—completely—and try to figure out a new way to accomplish the same end.

You won't get rid of 100 percent of the negatives, but you can start cleaning and make *some* progress.

Take sales for a moment. You're in a slump. You're not selling anybody. You haven't made any money. You owe the world money immediately. How can you be up? Well, here are some of the things you can do:

1. Imagine what the end looks like and keep it in mind.

2. Ask yourself, "How would I feel if the next three people that I'm going to see will buy from me?" What can you do to help give that a better chance of actually happening. Prospects don't want to see you down. Get yourself back up again by thinking that they're going to buy.

3. Act enthusiastically and focus on why it is to your prospect's genuine advantage to buy. Concentrate on the real benefit they will receive when they do buy.

4. *Be* enthusiastic when you go out and see them. Let them know that you believe what they're going to do is the right thing for them to do and, as they begin hearing you and feeling you, they'll buy.

5. Dream they'll buy—and they will buy—because they'll feel how much you believe that it's in their best interest to buy.

You can change your behavior, and that will change your mind. You'll have the kind of energy that prospects need to pick up on in order to decide to buy.

Now, once that works once for you, why not bring the same sense of urgency to the next opportunity? And the next, and then the one after that.

Make it a habit to make it urgent!

And things will begin to change in your life, as long as you keep thinking up and keep thinking high.

Great Scene #7

Dorothy again demonstrates that taking "no" for an answer is a concept she just doesn't want to understand. And she's not shy about letting people know how she feels. Learning to express yourself effectively is a value tool to have on your way to Successville.

In the next interesting development in the story, we see the crew skipping up to the gate and Dorothy ringing the bell, totally excited (kind of like how I was when arriving in Philadelphia!). A window cut into the door opens, and a man sticks his face out.

He's angry and wants to know who rang the bell. In unison, they all shout, "We did!" But the Doorman gets even angrier. He insists there's a notice by the doorbell button that says, "Out of Order."

But it turns out there is no notice posted. They tell him so. The Doorman looks and sees they are right. He goes back inside, gets a notice, and posts it. It reads, "Bell Out of Order. Please Knock!"

Then he slams the door.

I laughed out loud at this. This bit of business reminds me of a million incidents.

How many times have you been confronted with some petty person or rule that makes no sense—that only blocks your forward progress?

Well, I have a saying about that kind of obstacle: "Go 'round it, over it, under it—or go through it. Just keep going."

Anyway, after reading the silly sign, Dorothy does what it asks. She knocks. The man pops his head out from the window again.

Once more, he refuses to admit them and slams the door closed.

By the way, it's true that you can't win them all.

But I can guarantee this: you can win many times more than you've been winning.

Using the lessons available in *The Wizard of Oz*, I know you can dramatically increase the percentage of situations where you come out a winner.

Again, Dorothy knocks, and again the Doorman arrives. This time, though, Dorothy manages to tell him that the Good Witch of the North has sent her. She proves it by showing her ruby slippers.

That changes everything. But if Dorothy hadn't have hung in there, she never would have had the chance to tell the Doorman the one thing that got him to open the door.

Now, the Wicked Witch is still at it.

She flies overhead on her broom and cackles as a long streak of thick black smoke trails behind her, spelling out the letters:

S—U—R—R

All four of them look up. The Witch spells out the rest of her message: "Surrender Dorothy."

The words in the sky caused panic in the townspeople of the Emerald City. They rush to the Wizard for an explanation of the sky writing. But when they get there, they are met by an angry guard.

Right on the verge of meeting the Wizard, the ominous message appears: "Surrender Dorothy."

In other words, give up. Something bad is going to happen.

But Dorothy doesn't give up, does she?

What is the point here?

Practice at what you want to be.

Why start such a fantastic, dangerous journey in the first place if you're willing to chicken out and give up when things get rough.

Can it be that they're threatening you because they're afraid that your success will signal their own downfall or failure?

Good work, Dorothy!

Way to go!

By the way, a long time ago I learned that the advice "don't stifle your emotions" is worth taking. Now, I don't go around weeping when I go to see a client, but I'm not ashamed to share my grief and my joy with those I know. Sometimes my mind tells me to hide something, but my belly tells me to be natural. I almost always follow its advice.

Had Dorothy tried to hide her true nature, which was to cry in this situation, it's very likely that the severity of her plight would have gone unnoticed by the Guard.

Fantasy Power

I want to tell you a story about Capt. Jerry Coffee. I saw him speak once, and he told an amazing story.

Coffee was in the Korean War, during which he was captured and became a prisoner of war, a POW.

He spent six and one-half years in a cell about the size of a 4-by-8 room, most of the time in total darkness. He was in the most brutal form of solitary confinement.

Now, before he was captured, Coffee had played a little bit of golf in his life. Not too much, and he didn't play that well at all.

When Coffee was finally released, he went to a golf course, and what do you think happened?

I'll tell you: he was almost able to play scratch golf.

Why? What had happened? How did his mediocre golf game improve so dramatically despite the inhumane abuse he suffered?

He played every day in that cell.

Now how do you play golf in a 4-by-8 cell? You play it in your mind. You see the green, you see the tee. You feel the swing, you practice putting. Again and again and again and again. You note the slope of the hill in front of the hole. You make mistakes, you work on them. You improve your stance. You imagine how to change your swing if it's windy, or what you do if the sun's in your eyes.

Coffee came out almost a scratch golfer. Now, that is the power of the mind and dreaming in color.

Insight from Oz: What the mind can conceive, you can achieve. That's important. As long as you have a direction and know what you want to see, you can build it in your mind so clearly, so vividly, that it becomes real. Really real.

Words from the Wise
Valuable Insights about the Journey—from Successful People

I have learned this at least by my experiment: That if one advances confidently in the direction of his dreams, and endeavors to live the life which he has imagined, he will meet with a success unexpected in common hours.

Henry David Thoreau

Reality Is a Verb!

Deciding to Make Your Dream a Reality

To make your dream a reality, you must do the things that winners do—things that other people just won't do. They can do them—they just don't do them.

As frightened as Dorothy is, she forces herself to have the courage to approach the fiery Wizard—even after he tries to intimidate her and make her leave his chamber.

You must pay attention to all the small details. You have to become devoted to doing the things that you'd rather not do but that you know you must do. Whoever first said "the devil is in the details" was right. But the gold is in the details, too. Once you make the details a top priority, then you've conquered one of the keys to making your dream a reality.

Concentrating on the details is the start button. It is the button that says, "OK, I've decided. I'm going to do it. I'm going to succeed."

Until you definitely decide that you want to do it, it's not going to happen.

I just read Maxwell Maltz's book *Psycho-Cybernetics* again for the two-hundredth time this past weekend, and he says that you can have whatever you want *as long as you be sure to dream about it.* He says the unconscious mind and the conscious mind think completely alike.

Whether you are thinking and dreaming about something or actually doing it, there's no difference to the unconscious mind. In terms of impact, it has the same impact.

You can rehearse and rehearse and rehearse.

So if you can look at this chapter and decide to make your dream a reality, what you're really doing is beginning with the end in mind.

You know what you want to accomplish so clearly that you have a complete road map, that TripTik to get you there, and deciding to do it is the major step.

That's the start button to make it work.

Dreams vs. Goals

Now let's talk about pressing your Start button. You can dream all you want, but if you don't first press your Start button, nothing will happen.

Except you'll dream a lot.

The best way I know to press your start button is to convert your dream into a goal.

What's the difference between a dream and a goal?

Dreams and goals have one major difference: goals have deadlines.

Close this book for a moment (mark the page first, please) and think about the simple truth of that. Dreams are dreamy, but goals have deadlines.

> *Wizard Wisdom: Make a list of your goals and set reasonable, workable deadlines to get them accomplished.*

A goal has a fuse, and once you put a match to that fuse, it becomes a goal. It becomes an achievable goal. Otherwise, your goal is nothing more than a dream. It's "something I'd like to do when I get a chance someday."

Converting a dream into a goal is part of the evolutionary process of success.

Dreams and ideas don't exist physically. Achieving success consists of taking an idea that was born in your head and making it real. You have to give it substance and structure in the physical universe.

You have to give it form.

Develop Self-Discipline

Self-discipline is the motor that propels your boat. It guarantees you'll stay on the Yellow Brick Road—and you can take it anywhere you go.

You've got to have discipline to keep going when things get tough. *Dorothy never lets up.*

You can turn failure into success by having the discipline to get better. Just think of this formula:

Failure + Discipline = Success

Part of having discipline is having the will to try more. You'll lose more, but you'll win more, too. Here's another formula for success to remember:

Trying More = Losing More + Winning More

Always be ready.
Do what others do—just do more of it.
Be committed, persist, and your discipline will see you through.

> **Wizard Wisdom:** *Remember these three keys for success:* **discipline, persistence, commitment.** *Remind yourself again and again that you need these qualities for your success.*

> **Insight from Oz:** *Dream + Effort = Achievement*

An idea or dream pops into your head. You have to help the process along by adding the secret ingredient called *effort*. Maybe you call it *work*. Maybe you call it *discipline*. It doesn't matter what you call it as long as you do it. You add that critical ingredient by committing yourself to making that dream come true. By giving an idea a deadline, you light its fuse. And the difference between a dream floating around somewhere in your head and a solid accomplishment you can take to the bank is nothing more complicated than lighting that fuse.

Dream: Let's say two people are in love and they get married. They decide they want to have a baby. Raising a family has been a dream for both of them for a long time.

"When can we have our baby?" the man asks.

Deadline: "As soon as you graduate from school and can start working to support us," the woman says.

"But graduation's only a few months away, and I already have a job offer," he says.

Effort: "Then let's get to work and start making the baby!" she says.

Sticking to the plan is easier said than done, but that's what separates ordinary people from extraordinary people.

When we get to the section about deciding to make the dream a reality, you will realize that that's just as important as having the dream in the first place.

If you don't decide to decide, you are on Stuck.

If you don't decide to decide, you go no farther than where you are now.

When ordinary people have dreams and begin to dream those dreams in color, they put the dream in the context of a time frame. They begin to work that dream, and they continue working it on a regular basis.

That's when ordinary people transform themselves into extraordinary people. They use ordinary effort to accomplish extraordinary deeds. But they never let up. They persist, and if they can't get around something in their way, they'll go over it. Or under it. If need be, they'll go through it. But they won't let anything stop them.

What do I mean by using ordinary effort to accomplish extraordinary deeds?

Look at it this way: If a twelve-year-old-kid gets an odd job after school every day and decides that no matter what she's going to save $10 a week, do you know that by the time she's forty-two, she'll have accumulated more than $800,000!

That's what I mean by "using ordinary effort to accomplish extraordinary deeds."

It doesn't take a tremendously unbearable effort to go from ordinary to extraordinary. It does take dedication and commitment.

Think about the Hall of Fame baseball player, for example.

The Hall of Famer strikes out about two times for every one time he gets on base. And he's still a Hall of Famer. Wait a minute, you may say. How can that be? How can you strike out two out of three times and still be a giant success?

I don't know! But that's what the numbers say! Batting around .333 over a career can land you in the Hall of Fame. And that includes some really lame years you might have had.

And by the way, don't scorn the bad years you're bound to have no matter what line you are in. You will realize that you learn more from the failures than you do from the successes.

Your bad times are diagnostic. They point out the problems. You'd never grow without them. *But you'd be shocked at how many people quit and give up altogether because they have a bad streak or two, or three, or even four.* What's the Chinese saying? "Fall down seven times. Get up eight!"

Well, once you begin doing that—learning to persist—and once you begin pressing the Start button, you will go from being ordinary to extraordinary. You'll begin building a collection of wins.

Once you begin building that collection, you won't have to go to the Hall of Fame selection committee. The Hall of Fame selection committee will come to you. And if you're not home, don't worry. They'll wait for you!

And as you can begin doing that—making all those successes— you'll get more and more people to join you, to work with you, to work for you. You'll build a team—a winning team—and that will start to snowball.

And when that happens, do you know who you can thank?
You can thank yourself!

Obtain Your Goal by Creating Milestones

When you are planning a trip and you call AAA for one of those TripTiks they provide, the first thing you ask—the most important question you have—is: "How do I get there?"

That is Dorothy's first question, too.

Dorothy: But how do I start for Emerald City?
Glinda: It's always best to start at the beginning. And all you do is follow the Yellow Brick Road.

—from *The Wizard of Oz* screenplay

When you call AAA and say, "I'd like to go from New York to San Francisco. What's the best route?" they don't pull out one of those giant maps and unfold it all over a desk. They give you little sheets, little segments of a map. Then they take the little sheets and trace a route for you, using a highlighter to mark it, and show you the best way to get to where you want to go. It might take ten or twenty little sheets to get you there, but it does get you there.

Those sheets are just pieces of the big map cut up into pieces and bound together. So, as you turn the pages of the Triptik, you see a bite-sized piece at a time, with maybe about two or three hours' worth of travel on each sheet. It's not overwhelming; it's got all the specific entrances and exits and landmarks you need. And AAA also knows about any detours or other problems and routes you around them.

> ***Insight from Oz:*** *It's a cinch by the inch, but hard by the yard.*

So they give you little bite-size pieces.

I guess they must have discovered that the giant map is too hard to work with, to hard to look at, too much to look at, all at one time. You can achieve success the same way you eat a meal or drive across the country: one bite at a time.

When you are finished with one piece, you turn to the next page that takes over where the other left off. You do this over and over again until you get to where you wanted to go.

People have a lot of problems with getting started on something because they view the job as being too big, too overwhelming.

Viewing the whole thing is good. You need to do that. That's how you establish your goal. But that is not how you achieve it.

Once you have the goal down in your mind, and it's vivid, and it's in color, and you can visualize the trip, you go to your own internal AAA. You go to your brain.

Make up a Triptik of what you want to accomplish. Really. Put it down on paper. Break it down into tiny, simpler tasks. Be sure that each task, once completed, contributes to getting you closer and closer to your goal. Some completed tasks may make huge contributions, and other tasks may seem like they are hardly worth it. Break it down, once you see the whole picture, into individual sheets. Begin to do one task at a time. Give each project a deadline, but be sure it is a reasonable deadline. If you make unreasonable deadlines, you may be setting yourself up with an easy out. "I can't do that! That's impossible! I must have been crazy to think I could pull that off!"

Now, once you have been able break the whole thing into the bite-sized pieces and only worry about one bite-sized piece at a time, keeping in mind the goal of going the whole route, things get easier—and the quality of the results are better.

On the other hand, if you're worrying about the whole three-thousand-mile trip, the whole scene will be too much. The same principle applies in earning a living or in doing anything else.

The smart people, who want to take control of themselves, take the whole job, break it into manageable pieces, and put a piece here, and a piece here, and a piece here. That way, they can keep control of all of it, look at all of it, but focus on one piece at a time.

Before you know it, you've got half of it finished. Then, 60 percent is finished, the 70 percent, then 80 percent, then, 90 percent is done. And, during the whole process, you are constantly modifying, correcting, and rethinking all the time.

If you get to a roadblock, you go around it.

And then the next thing you know, it's completed.

So, one gigantic job—impossible to deal with as a whole—is nothing more than a series of simple, easy-to-deal-with projects. Make this call, write that report. See this person, get that information. Get this approved, double-check on that. Correct this mistake, delegate that task.

Remember, you can't do everything.

But you sure can do *anything*.

All of this is part of managing yourself, disciplining yourself, pressing the start button.

But if you don't approach big problems this way, you will accomplish nothing, and you'll say, "The job's too big. I can't do it."

And you may not even say that. You just may think that and never even try at all.

And that's why sometimes you wake up in the morning and fail to act on what you promised yourself you would do the night before. You think a job is too big. You think it is bigger than you.

Once you've broken it into pieces, look over all the parts and pick the best one to begin with.

And press that Start button.

More Trade Secrets

The Fact Finder

Fact finders are checklists that help you learn every single thing you need to know about a prospect's personal and financial situation.

You can get a fact finder checklist practically everywhere. If your insurance company or agency doesn't have one, write to me and I'll send you one.

Learn to build a dossier on your prospect.

Your instincts are instrumental when assessing if your client can afford your product—just from the feel of it when you first meet somebody. You have a feel for whether you are in the wrong place or the right place.

Fact finding means that you ask a lot of questions to try to get as much information as you can about the prospect, both personal and financial.

A fact-finding session helps you to learn whether or not a prospect can afford to buy.

You have a checklist—a fact finder—and by going through that fact finder and asking the questions that are listed, you are going to get responses that will clue you in to much more than meets the eye.

The prospect's answers to simple questions will speak volumes. But it is up to you to conduct enough of these fact-finding sessions to get good at "diagnosing" the situation.

It becomes instinctive, and I can't tell you how to develop those instincts. But I can promise you that if you make fact finding a priority, you'll get very good at interpreting the responses.

The next thing you know, you'll have developed the instincts.

The fact finder gives you a track to run on and doesn't let you stray from what you want to learn. I can't forget anything because it's right there in black and white.

The fact finder will help you identify the size of the problem that's standing between you and a sale—if there are any problems. Sometimes it's just a breeze.

The size of the problem is important. If someone only needs $50,000 in life insurance, I pass the case on to one of the new kids. It's too small for me. Maybe not for you, based on where you are in your career, but for me, I have bigger fish to fry.

So, the fact finder identifies the size of the problem and the type of need (whether it is a estate tax need, a buy/sell need, or something else) so that then I have something I can sink my teeth into. I started out without any information except some guy's phone number, and now I know more about his need for insurance than he does.

Now I have something I can sell.

Begin with the End in Mind

The picture of what you want to accomplish in the end—your goal—has to be vivid in your mind. That way, you know what you are shooting for.

To Dorothy, the visions of Auntie Em's farm back in Kansas are pretty clear. She knows what she wants and knows what it is she has to do in order to get it.

There's no point in starting unless you know what you want something to look like when you finish. If you don't know what the end looks like, you never get there. You won't be able to make those little corrections and adjustments along the way because you don't know what you are looking for.

In my company, if we like to do $3 million in commissions, but if we don't know what it looks like and feels like and exactly what we have to do each day, each week, each month, each quarter in order to get to that goal, we never would be able to get there. And getting to $3 million costs us money. It creates expenses in expense accounts and expense allowances, and we have to know the cost of doing business. If we don't know our goal, how can we ever control our expenses?

But the planning process comes first. You set up your goal, and you say, "I want to $3 million in sales this year." You say you want to be profitable, you want to attract certain new brokers, you want to have a certain discipline in the office to get things done.

All of this is part of the big picture. Once you have that, then you can go back and break it down into bite-sized pieces and get those little pieces done one piece at a time.

For example, let's assume someone wants to achieve a certain sales goal—say, reaching the Million Dollar Round Table. And the qualifying for the MDRT means earning $50,000 in first-year commissions to get there.

Well, the first step is saying, "I want to make the MDRT."

That's the big picture, being able to say, "I'd like to make the Round Table this year."

When he analyzes it, he says to himself, "Listen, to get to the MDRT, it's got to be $50,000 in first-year commissions. Now I must determine what are the steps? What is the plan to get there? Well, if I broke it down by the month, I need about $4,156. And if I did that every month, by the end of the year I need about $1,000 a week. For the four weeks, that would make the month and make the year."

But the most important thing that I must know is that I want to make the MDRT, and I must know that I want to have $50,000 in first-year commissions. That's the big plan.

As simple as all of this sounds, lots of people don't do it.

They get up in the morning and say, "I'd like to make the MDRT this year. I didn't do it last year, but I want to do it this year."

But that's where it stops.

It is a dream, not a goal.

And the difference between a dream and a goal is what? Merely a date. You put a date to it, then a dream becomes a goal.

If you fail to stick to your goal, at least you know what went wrong, At least you can point to some specific behavior of yours—or lack of behavior—that caused the problem. You may choose to correct it, or you may choose to ignore it. But by having made a goal, you've made a lot of progress over just having a dream.

That's the first key of managing yourself in relationship to time: knowing exactly where you want to go and knowing exactly what you have to do to get there.

More Trade Secrets

Callbacks

When you don't get the sale, unless you can tell it's a definite mismatch of personalities, there's no reason—except frail ego—not to go back there.

Remember when Dorothy first gets to the Wizard's place? The guard refuses to let her in. She is upset—but that doesn't stop her. She bangs that big brass door knocker again and again until the guard finally relents. Someone shyer would have slithered away.

But not Dorothy. She makes her callback. And it pays off.

Many times people don't buy because they are not ready to, or they bought elsewhere because they have a brother-in-law in the business. It wasn't a matter of someone else having a better price or a better product. You just are not going to get the busies for circumstances that have nothing to do with you.

When you strike out, send out a "thank-you" letter for having had the opportunity to bid on the business and to get to know that person. Then go another step further and put the letter in a file to follow upon maybe six months down the road.

Although that prospect has bought nothing today, six months down the road, if the right scenario develops, the prospect may be very warm, and in a sense, your call is like a referral, because the prospect already knows you doesn't have an uncomfortable feeling about you because of the note you sent. You can walk in again and make a sale or get a referral.

 # Great Scene #8

The Lion becomes paralyzed in fear when he thinks someone has yanked his tail—but he has done it to himself. In my own life, I'd have much more money if I had a dollar for every time I've looked around for someone to blame when things were going wrong in my life. The culprit was right there, staring at me from my bathroom mirror. What about you?

When we last left Dorothy and the crew, Dorothy had succeeded in getting the Doorman to let them in, despite his instructions to the contrary.

The guard slips out of view, but in a moment, the doors of the palace creak open. Entering in awe and silence, the crew goes down a long corridor with high ceilings.

Suddenly, the Lion's weakness asserts itself. He says he's been thinking about it and maybe it isn't such a good idea after all that he goes in.

Dorothy reminds him that the Wizard will give him the courage he needs. At this point, the Lion calms down and absent-mindedly wipes away his tears with the end of his tail.

He turns to run, but they stop him.

As they stand talking, the lion unthinkingly tugs at his tail. He screams in panic.

The Scarecrow wants to know what's wrong.

The Lion cowers and whines that someone has pulled his tail.

The Scarecrow tells him that he has pulled his own tail.

The Lion recognizes what has happened.

How often do we do that to ourselves? How many times have you pulled your own tail, only to assume someone did it?

Face It! Or, Avoiding Avoidance

Make a list of those things in your life that you're not facing.

Wouldn't you be better served by jumping in feet first and confronting even one of them?

Pick one and put it on your checklist today.

Wizard Wisdom: *The more you act, the less you have to react.*

Remember Your Dreams—in Vivid Detail

I've heard people say at sales meetings that although they weren't winning sales contests, they started picturing themselves actually attending the meetings where the winners go—usually some great resort, maybe Hawaii—sitting in a chair and watching the opening session, even though they've never been there before.

By dreaming about it and thinking about it, they unconsciously create behavior that leads to their winning the contests.

Why?

Because they wanted to be a part of the picture they had in their mind.

It's been said so many times that what the mind can conceive, you can achieve. If you can see yourself doing something, if you envision it hard enough and long enough, it will happen. You break through the barrier between the unconscious mind and the conscious mind.

You don't know the difference, it seems real, and you find yourself working toward it.

If you can believe it, and see it in your mind enough, you can actually achieve it. If it is something you want—something you really want badly enough, you get it.

Obstacles along the Way

The fact of the matter is that you cannot manage time.

Time moves at an even pace, whether you like it or not. You can't make it go faster, and you can't slow it down.

The best you can do is to manage *you* within a time frame. And once you've got a plan, you want to implement the plan within the boundaries of the time frame you have established.

So let's say that now that you've got your steps laid out and you know how you're going to achieve that plan. How you are going to get from where you are to that goal?

But now comes the biggest part of the problem, if it can be called a problem. How do you manage yourself to get to do the things you promised yourself you would do the night before?

You lie in bed at night and say, "Tomorrow morning, I'm gonna get up and start."

And then the next morning comes, and you get up—and you don't do anything.

What gets in the way?

Take Action for Success!: *Think about that. Write down every excuse you use to get out of doing what you promised yourself you'd do. Make a list. You'll see a pattern. What is it?*

Motivation and Your Dream

It's like Larry Wilson of Wilson Learning Corporation said to us many years ago; "People do things for *their* reasons—not *our* reasons."

You can't motivate anybody to do anything. You can only motivate them to motivate themselves. Only they can motivate themselves.

They have to have that picture in their mind, and that is what this planning process is all about: having a picture in mind that is so clear that when they achieve their goal, they will know, definitely, that it's what they always wanted.

They will have become so familiar with that image of what they want that it will just be plainly obvious.

If that isn't that clear, they're not going to get it, and even if they stumble upon it, they won't recognize it anyway.

Stop! And Evaluate Your Progress

I heard Joe Waldon say that jet pilots don't use rearview mirrors. And I think he's right. There is no rearview mirror on a jet plane. A pilot can't look back. A pilot doesn't need to look back. Because he's going too fast, he has to look forward. And he only can go forward.

But every once in a while, he does land to evaluate what's going on. That's when he inspects his aircraft—once he's slowed down. His inspections are planned. They don't happen whenever he feels like it (unless there's an emergency, but that's a different story). They don't come up as convenient excuses to avoid flying. Inspections are critically important. But they are planned.

And once an inspection is complete, the pilot takes off again.

Maybe that's what most of us have got to do more often—land. When we are up in the air, we ought to go like mad.

Make sure you're going in the right direction. Make sure you are going as fast as you can and have all the things you need, and then go like mad. But then you will eventually have to land and make an evaluation.

And that's what I mean about putting it in neutral every once in a while.

I don't think the problem is that most people don't land.

I think it's that most people don't take off.

But of those who do take off, less than one-tenth of 1 percent actually go on to become extraordinary, to do extraordinary things. And yet, at the heart of it all, they are just ordinary people—doing extraordinary things.

Those successful people take off, fly very fast, and come down for a landing. And when they get a little bit tired, they take a break, reevaluate, reassess, take off again, and go like mad.

Everybody else is just flopping around, sometimes crashing, sometimes flying, sometimes out of control, going faster than a plane ought to go.

But essentially, it's like the turtle and the hare again.

Generally, it's the hare that's going up and down, flying, first really fast and then barely moving all at. No destination, no place to go—as opposed to the turtle, who makes up his mind about what he wants, sticks his neck out first (because he can't go anywhere until he puts his neck out), and then continues going, slowly, steadily, until he comes across the finish line.

> ***Take Action for Success!:*** *Constantly ask yourself, "Where am I now? Where do I want to go? How will I get there? What are the checkpoints along the way?" If you can't do that, you shouldn't begin. You have to sit tight and think about those things.*

The Planning Process

Some plans design themselves, while other plans need deep thought and lots of brainstorming. For Dorothy, the Scarecrow, the Lion, and the Tin Man, the plan is obvious. All they have to do is to work it. That—and only that—it exactly why they all get everything they set out for: a return to Kansas, brains, courage, and a heart.

Now, let's move from fiction to reality.

Let's say I decide that I want to earn $1,000 in commissions each week.

If my family requires $50,000 a year, then I need to live on a budget of $1,000 a week. It's simple.

I then use my planning process to answer the question: "How do I get 50 grand?"

That's the first step: I need 50 grand.

If I don't know that I need the 50 grand—my goal—then what's the point in getting started? I won't know where I'm going. Being vague is counterproductive. There's a world of difference between saying, "I need to make a lot of money," and "I need to make 50 grand during the next fifty-two weeks." The first statement is a dream; the second is a specific, definite, time-framed goal, something you can get your arms around.

Or let's say I know I need more salespeople. That's the dream. Now, I make it into a goal. I want to hire several recruits this year, but I have to know exactly how many I want. I come up with the number seven. Why do I want seven?

I want seven because from experience I know I will earn an average of $7,000 from each and I want 50 grand of first-year commissions from that group.

I know I have to ask around to see if any of my salespeople know of any other salespeople I might want to interview.

Now, how do I actually get the seven?

What are the individual steps I need to take, from getting candidates to interviewing them, to actually getting them out on the street with my agency's applications in their pockets?

I put the planning process at the very beginning—not halfway down the road.

I want to have the end in mind. I know what I want to accomplish. You have to know what you want *before* you begin.

When I tell people these things, every now and then someone will say, "Sid, it's so obvious. It's so simple!"

I know.

But that doesn't make it popular. So many people don't do these simple, obvious things. If you do them, your life will change dramatically—for the better.

These same principles apply to everything. *Everything!*

Even having children. You can plan that when you're getting married. "I'd like to have two children, three children in this marriage. And then you begin the plan of having two or three children. When can I have them? How will I pay for the things they'll need? What does my wife want? Is the house big enough? If not, when will we need to move?"

All this planning is not robbing me of being spontaneous. It's actually helping me. I'm giving myself—and my family—the tools to do whatever we want. I'm examining the possibilities.

"I want a house with a white picket fence," you say, and you begin working toward a goal of saving enough money for that house with a white picket fence.

But you have to know you want the house; you have to know what it looks like.

That's the soul of the planning process: to avoid getting a surprise, to have the end in mind before you begin so you can make a plan to get to where you want to go.

And that applies to your business, your personal life, your family life, and your kids—everything.

More Trade Secrets

Display Interest in Your Client

When I display interest, my client (or prospect) knows I care. As I always say, caring is very important in the discovery process. The more a client can feel that you care, the more he or she will let you in. And that helps the all-important discovery process.

The more you know, the more everybody can win. The more information you get, the easier it is for you to solve the problem.

Once I understand a problem, the solution just jumps out. And generally the client is interested in the solution.

So in addition to getting a Dun & Bradstreet financial report on your prospect, you might go to his accountant and attorney—with permission of course—and maybe other people who might know him, so that you can learn more about the person and the business.

The more discovery information you get, the easier it is to find the problem—and then the solution.

I'm talking about life insurance in this case, but the fact is that this could be cars or real estate or anything, right?

Selling is selling is selling, isn't it?

People always buy for the same basic reasons: the salesperson knows the problem and has the solution.

It's really that simple. The trick is in getting the details right.

Do What You Really Like

How hard is it for Dorothy to grab Toto and head for the hills in the beginning of the story?

It is easy. She doesn't even have to think about it. She is doing what she wants to do. There's a great lesson there.

I work about one hundred hours week, do dozens of different activities, and do you know what? I don't have even one thing that I hate to do. Well, that's not exactly true. Many times I don't like going to the gym to work out. But I go. I can afford to send someone to go for me, but somehow that loses something in the translation. But other than the gym, there is nothing I do not like doing.

If you forced me to tell you what I like doing the least out of all the things I do, I'd answer your question, but I don't really hate anything I do. I'd tell you I don't like making cold phone calls. I don't like calling strangers on the phone asking for appointments, so I don't do it very much. But in the days when I needed to do it, I found a way to love doing it.

I explained to myself that if I earned $100,000 during the course of a year, and that if I stuck to my goal of making twenty cold calls each week, it would work out that each call—successful or a hang-up in my face—would be worth $96.15! Imagine that: getting paid $96 for someone to say, "Forget it!" and hang up on me.

See what I mean. When cold calling was what I needed to do, I found a way to genuinely enjoy it! And I'm not that smart! You can probably find even better ways to enjoy the things you have to do.

Today, I don't need to do it. I still need new business, but I just find other ways to get it. I use direct mail. I use telemarketers.

I guess this is what I'm trying to tell you: Don't do what you don't want. Do what you like to do and make it work.

Where is it written that you've got to do things you hate? Where is it written that you shouldn't love what you do?

If you don't like something, find another avenue.

It's like your heart. You have arteries and veins that blood comes through and from. The heart knows pretty quickly if one of the veins gets blocked. But it doesn't just stop. It finds a new path. It gets around the blockage.

Now, if too many blockages occur, you have yourself a heart attack. Planning and keeping to your goals will prevent that major shutdown, but if that doesn't happen, the blood finds alternate ways to circulate and keep moving all those parts around in your body.

Do the same thing with your life!

There are things I like better than others, but there's nothing that I don't like. Nothing. I don't have anything on my plate that I really hate. I got rid of it. I enjoy the whole thing.

Of course, I don't like it when a prospect says no, but that's not all the time, thank God.

Words from the Wise
Valuable Insights about the Journey—from Successful People

I once worked for a builder of houses, and one day I went with him when he visited a piece of ground where he planned to build. I watched him walk over the ground. I watched him check the depth of nearby water. I saw him work and rework building plans. A closet was sketched in, then erased. A bathroom was moved and removed in the blueprint. The final positioning of the house on the lot was changed and changed again. There were calls to the electric company and the gas company and the title company. A week later, he was still fussing over the details. I finally asked him, "When do we get to work and begin building?" "Building!" he said. "That's the easy part. What we are doing now—the planning—this is the real work!"

In my speaking engagements around the world, people see me stroll up to the stage, talk for an hour, show some slides and maybe a video, and then walk off.

"Gee, speaking looks easy," someone once told me after I had spoken. He was right: the speaking part is the easy part. What he didn't see are the months of planning, researching, writing, rewriting, telephone calling, and double-checking that go into each show. I once calculated that each minute of speaking takes about one hour of preparation. An hourlong presentation can easily take a full week and a half to properly prepare. When I go to speak, I study the things I know will be relevant for my audience. No matter what kind of group I'm addressing, I study their nomenclature, problems, successes, and failures. I know them, and I know what is meaningful to them. And that is why I am invited to speak so often."

—Murray Raphel

Great Scene #9

Despite incredible odds, Dorothy and the crew best both the Wizard and the Wicked Witch. They succeed because they have a goal, have motivation, and will not give up! The most massive mountain ranges in the world are worn down to mere hills over time by nothing more than the persistence of a gentle breeze. Never let up.

The crew enters the great hall where the Wizard is. Oz's booming voice beckons them to come forward.

They are terrified. They stare at a giant head floating above the throne. On either side of the throne are two silver urns spewing smoke and fire. Oz's voice booms out, identifying himself as the "great and powerful."

They explain who they are and what they want.

But Oz isn't easy to deal with. He gives them a seemingly impossible task: recover the witch's broomstick.

They crew is terrified at the prospect of having to do this. They leave the palace, hoping to do as Oz commanded.

But guess what?

The Wicked Witch, observing them through her crystal ball, steps in, telling the flying monkeys to go kidnap Dorothy and Toto.

The flying monkeys grab hold of Dorothy and Toto.

They leave the other three crew members behind.

Toto is put in the same basket that Elmira Gulch had earlier in the movie. The Witch mutters the same words Elmira Gulch did about wanting Toto.

And when Toto is threatened, Dorothy is ready to trade her ruby slippers—her power—for Toto's life, even though she knows that it will cost her her life to remove them.

Once again, Toto jumps out of a basket (you gotta love that dog!) and distracts the Witch's attention from Dorothy.

The guards go after Toto, but they can't grab him.

Dorothy is with the Witch and keeps saying how scared she is. "Help me!" she cries, and then the image of Auntie Em appears in the crystal ball.

I think the point of this scene is that if you are in trouble or need help, don't be shy about it. Let it be known. People who love you and care about you will come to your aid.

But before you can ask for help, you have to recognize that you need it. This is really important. Admit it to yourself, because if you can't admit it to yourself, then how can you ask anyone else to help you?

The Lion, who normally is scared out of his wits over anything, is somehow willing to risk anything to go help Dorothy.

What is happening?

As scared as he is, he isn't too scared to go help her.

He is able to overcome his problem because he is motivated to help someone else! It's like the story of the man who finds a child pinned under a car and can somehow lift the car up with one hand and pull the kid out with the other!

Strength comes to us when we need it, generally only if we are motivated by something positive.

The more motivation you have, the easier it is to carry on.

So, one extremely important tool we learn from the Lion is to learn how to motivate yourself.

By running as fast as he can, Toto makes it back to the rest of the crew and leads them to the castle, where Dorothy is being held.

They are intent on saving her.

The Scarecrow comes up with the plan, and the Cowardly Lion (beginning already to change into a more courageous being) is scared but agrees to help anyway. The Lion, who has already proven he's afraid of his own roar, sees the importance of rescuing Dorothy—even at his own expense.

To me, this proves that if the goal is important to you, then there is nothing that is too frightening or scary to go through in order to achieve it.

They make their way back to the Witch's castle, where they meet a serious obstacle. They are captured by the Witch, who threatens to destroy them all, starting with the Scarecrow. The Witch also takes Toto and puts him in a basket. Dorothy screams at her to give Toto back.

The Witch refuses—unless Dorothy hands over the slippers.

Dorothy says she was warned by the Good Witch not to remove them.

The Witch threatens to throw the basket into the river and drown the dog.

In order to save Toto (again), Dorothy relents. But when the Witch bends down to take the slippers—she can't touch those slippers—they're too hot and burn her hands. The Witch says she should have realized the slippers will never come off while Dorothy's still alive. A master of timing, Toto uses the distraction to escape.

The Wicked Witch starts an hourglass running and tells Dorothy, "This is how much longer you have to be alive."

Dorothy sees a distraught Auntie Em in the Witch's crystal ball.

Toto finds the Tin Man, the Scarecrow and the Lion in a forest and leads them over a difficult course back to the Witch's castle. The crew overpowers some guards, takes their costumes, and sneaks into the castle. They break into the room Dorothy's locked in just as the hourglass expires.

Then the Witch and the Winkie guards corner them.

The Scarecrow drops a chandelier on the legion of guards. Dorothy and her crew run but are recaptured. In an act of cruelty, the Witch jabs a blazing broomstick at the Scarecrow, causing the straw in his arm to catch fire.

He's screaming, and Dorothy's screaming. Spotting a bucket of water, Dorothy puts Toto down and grabs the bucket. The Witch, seeing what's about to happen, screams.

Dorothy tosses the water on the Scarecrow, but some of it misses and catches the Witch full in the face. It puts out the fire.

The Witch yelps in agony as she shrinks and shrivels.

She shrieks and then melts away into a puddle.

Well. That's the end of that.

Dorothy, the Tin Man, the Scarecrow, even Toto, look down, amazed at what they see: the Witch is now nothing more than a smoldering cloak and hat in a puddle on the floor. Toto goes over to inspect. Pawing at what used to be the witch, he sniffs until he's finally satisfied that she's gone.

The leader of the Winkies approaches Dorothy and reveals to her what a wonderful thing she's done for them by killing the Witch. Now they are free.

Time Barely Exists in the Land of Oz

Have you ever noticed how time sort of stands still in *The Wizard of Oz?*

You don't see any of the crew checking their watches. They're not following much of a schedule.

Have you ever thought about why?

Maybe it's because the crew is so intent on reaching their goal that time doesn't matter to them.

When does time drag? When you are bored or frustrated.

When does time fly? When you are so totally into something that time practically ceases to exist.

Have you have heard of the term *time management?* Well, try this theory: time doesn't need any managing—it does very well by itself. It's we people who need management.

Have you ever wondered why some people never seem to have enough time, while other people have too much time?

Well, we all have the same amount, at least as far as I know. Most of us have about twenty-four hours a day to work with.

And all we have to do is use it to the fullest so we can get the most out of the time that's available to us.

Here's a thought: We only have about a thousand months to live our lives.

If you're counting, that's about eighty-three and one-third years.

If you're fifty years old, you've already used 600 of those months. After having used 600, and with only 400 more to go, it would seem to me that we would make the best possible use of time that we possibly can—use as much as we can in the best way we can to make things happen for us.

My recommendation is to use that time in the most efficient way. In this chapter we'll talk about time and how to use it.

Managing Your ~~Time~~ Self

There are many kinds of time that we have to deal with, depending on who you are in your position in your career or what role you play in your home.

This is not only for business; this is the home.

There is boss-imposed time, self-imposed time, as well as other kinds of time.

For the moment, just take those two. You have self-imposed time: the things you have to give yourself a deadline for, the things you want to do. And you figure them out, you write them in your book, and you say, "I have to get this done before I go home today or before I go to sleep tonight."

Then there is "boss-imposed" time, which you have to put up with, and even though you have your plan laid out, the boss will inevitably come in and say, "Hey, would you do me a favor? Would you contact so-and-so and find out about next Thursday?"

Well, now all of a sudden that thing takes priority over what you are doing, and now you have to put your self-imposed stuff away for the boss-imposed thing. Of course, what makes life exciting is that you don't even know when boss-imposed stuff is going to happen to you.

Now, boss-imposed things may come from anyone, not only your actual boss from work. Anyone or anything who has the ability to influence you can be your boss if what they want or need is important to you. It may happen with your children or your wife. You may come home at night, planning to read a book, watch some TV, have some dinner, and play with the kids, and suddenly your wife says, "Listen, we have to go. I forgot to tell you that we have to go to a party at Charlie's mother's cousin's aunt's neighbor's."

What can you do? You love your wife, you want to compromise, so you go. You were planning to take it easy and go to sleep, and then

you find that you have to go out. So sometimes things get in the way.
Be sure to build time into your schedule for boss-imposed time.
It'll definitely happen.

The Concept of Time

Time waits for no one, and it won't wait for you.
—Mick Jagger and Keith Richards, The Rolling Stones

I want to talk about time—not traditional time management, but about the concept of time itself.

How you manage time is simply a matter of technique. But mastering time results from understanding it as a concept.

An old wise man once said, "Nature invented time so that everything wouldn't happen all at once."

Well, Nature succeeded beautifully. Things happen in sequence.

And people determined to be successful learn to take advantage of their ability to manipulate the sequence of events that they experience. People determined to be successful know they can't control everything, but by combining an understanding of time with strong self-discipline, they've really got a handle on something that makes a difference.

Time Is Continuous—Watch It Continually

The *Random House Webster's Unabridged Dictionary* takes more than eleven hundred words to explain sixty-four different definitions of the word "time." But I think the point is made in just a few words. Time is "the continuous duration . . . in which events succeed one another." I think the most important part of the definition is the word "continuous." Time never stops. It is a river always flowing past you. You can, by how you manipulate time, use it to carry you where you want to go. Or, by letting it manipulate you, you can drown in it.

Time, as I use it here, is a noun, and that means that it is a thing. Maybe you can't see it or touch it or taste it, but one thing is for sure: it exists, and it can be your ally or your adversary. How you get along with time is your choice. The beautiful thing is that, unlike most problems in life, changing time from a handicap to an advantage is a snap.

Organization, scheduling, time management, prioritization—they're different words, but they're all the same idea. In order to be successful, you need to master time. The most important thing you can do in business is manage—manage yourself. If you can get good at managing yourself, you'll soon see how to transfer that skill to other areas. You'll be better at managing your schedule, your business, your finances, your personal life, and your other pursuits.

And time is the key ingredient that differentiates between being ordinary and being extraordinary. That's the one common ingredient that makes superstars out of ordinary people.

You may wonder how time affects a classic superstar like a Michael Jordan. What makes him so good? How does time affect him? After all, he's just throwing the ball in the basket. That's not timing—or is it?

I think it is nothing but timing! How? Well, it took hours and hours and hours and hours and hours and hours of endless persistence and discipline to keep throwing that ball in the basket until one day Michael Jordan found himself in the NBA. To the typical sports fan, he just chucks that basketball toward the basket and it swishes through. It's a difficult thing to do, making that shot from halfway down the court. Maybe it looks so easy, but it took him twenty-five years to get there. Time and that other critical factor, discipline, have put him over the top.

The fact of the matter is that nothing in your life will get done without a proper understanding of the phenomenon we call time.

Preparation Is the Key

*Our plans miscarry because they have no aim. When a man
does not know what harbor he is making, no wind is the right wind.*
—Seneca, 4 B.C.

I've heard that Abraham Lincoln once said something like, "If you have eight hours to chop down a tree, spend six of them sharpening your axe."

In other words, spend time preparing. That's so terribly important in whatever you're going to do. Make sure that you're ready for the task at hand.

When you know what it is you want, your prep time decreases dramatically. The advice to "follow the Yellow Brick Road" is all the prepping Dorothy needs. Because her goal is clear, her course of action is obvious.

And being ready doesn't come easily. Even preparation has to be planned. The only way you can get to everything you have to do is by having the proper way to keep track of everything—the big projects and the little details.

One of the ways I keep track is via a time-management book. It doesn't matter if it is DayTimer, Franklin Planner, DayRunner, or even something you put together yourself. There are several excellent organizer systems that run on personal computers, too. Which system you use doesn't matter—as long as you use some system.

As I've said earlier, time management is merely a technique. Using time to your advantage is the fundamental strategy.

> **Wizard Wisdom:** *If you are not now using a time-management system, stop whatever it is you are doing and go get one. Office-supply stores, book shops, stationery dealers, and computer stores all carry a variety of systems. They can cost as little as $10 for a simple daily planner to hundreds of dollars for integrated hard-copy and computer-based systems.*

> **Insight from Oz:** *If you are just getting organized for the first time (or just getting reorganized after letting things get chaotic), be sure to block out plenty of time for this activity. Make certain that you have at least four full hours of uninterrupted, phones-off time to make the first sweep in organizing the mess on your desk and creating a list of priorities.*

The 62-Week Year

People always say to me, "If only I had more time." Well, as you know, we all have all the time there is. You can't make time go faster; you can't slow it down. Time goes the way time goes.

But you can, maybe mystically, get a 62-week year contained in a 52-week year.

A 62-week year is a good thing to have compared with the 52-week year most people say they work. However, most people don't work anywhere near 52 weeks each year.

But assuming you do, you probably in that 52-week year do what you're going to do but don't get maximum effectiveness and only wish you had more time.

Well, we've already learned that we have no more time. We can't make any more time from what time is, but there are certain things we can do to give ourselves more time.

For example, assume that you wake up 1 hour earlier in the morning. If you normally get up at 7, get up at 6 and work 1 more hour at night.

If you work 1 more hour in the morning and 1 more hour at night, that's another 2 hours every day of your life. It won't make a critical difference to each day, but look what it can do to a month, a quarter, or a year.

One more hour in the morning and 1 more hour at night is 2 hours a day times 5 days a week, so you'd be working 10 hours more each week.

If you do that and multiply 10 hours a week times 52 weeks, you're working another 520 hours every year. Now, if you divide 520 hours by the standard 40-hour workweek, you'll have 13 more weeks of productivity. Subtract three weeks for vacation, holidays, or sick time and you've achieved your 62-week year with flying colors.

Unclutter That Desk

Almost every person I meet has a cluttered desk—and that is a symptom of a cluttered mind. However, you can unclutter your mind as simply as you can unclutter your desk!

They go together. When your desk is all cluttered, the first thing you see in the morning in your office is your desk strewn full of papers. I can see how your mind *would* be totally cluttered and locked up. That's the way it goes. Keeping a cluttered desk doesn't make any sense to me.

On the other hand, if you come in and see your desk perfectly spotlessly clean, with everything in its place, you have to come ready for business that morning. Your mind has to be completely clear.

Mobile University

Do you have a high-tech tape recorder? I have a great one. It's called a VSC, for "variable-speed cassette" recorder.

It's a tape recorder that plays a tape 33 percent faster than a normal tape player can, which means that you can listen to an hour tape in about thirty-five minutes.

In order to avoid voices sounding like the Munchkins', there's a special feature on it that controls the voice pitch while playing the tape at a faster rate than normal players.

You listen to more in less time, and through the magic of your car's cigarette lighter, you become a mobile university, communing with the minds of success mentors past and present.

With a VSC tape player, you can put more information into your head so much more quickly. But even using a normal car tape player, you can absorb the success lessons of hundreds of extraordinary people.

Computers

Do you have a computer on your desk?

Do you own a simple, easy-to-use data-management system or data-capturing system? A place where you can put all the information down so you can retrieve it at any given time?

The personal computer has become the most revolutionary business tool of our time, and without one, you're missing out on an effective way to manipulate crucial personal and business information and organize your life. So look into getting one.

Scheduling Quiet Time

Are your phone calls made and taken at all hours of the day? Or do you have private time for yourself, quiet time, during which you take no phone calls and return phone calls at a future time?

Improve Your Problem-Solving Skills

Don't sit there and do nothing.

Do something.

You see, if you do something, you've done something, but if you do nothing, you've also done something: you've done nothing!

Here's a problem-solving problem: it isn't the problem that's the problem, it's the size of the problem that's the problem.

What kind of things do you do consistently to solve problems, even though you know they just won't work?

For your Success checklist, make a list of alternative responses to the situations that come up again and again that you never seem to resolve favorably. Then ask yourself *why* you keep doing them.

On the checklist, give yourself an assignment to use one of the alternative methods to solve your problem. If it doesn't work, would you be any worse off than you are now?

Great Scene #10

The Wizard is revealed as a fraud, but he also reveals his wisdom. The Scarecrow, the Tin Man, and the Cowardly Lion learn that they've always had what they thought they were lacking. But what about Dorothy?

They crew hurries back to the Wizard's throne room, Dorothy, Scarecrow, Lion, Tin Man and Toto face the throne, trembling, just like the first time they were there.

The floating head somehow frightens them even more this time.

Oz can't believe they have returned. And he's even more amazed to find they've achieved the goal he set for them.

Dorothy presses him to keep his promise. He stalls and tells her to come back tomorrow.

Toto senses something's out of whack. (Good dog, Toto. Good dog!) He sniffs at a curtain draped around the side of the throne.

The Wizard senses Toto's presence and tries to rush them all out of there, insisting they come back the following day.

Too late. Toto uses his teeth to pull the curtain aside. The Wizard is revealed with his back to the crew. He's unaware everyone can see him talking into a microphone.

The man looks over his shoulder to see the curtain has been pulled back by the dog. Dorothy moves forward—she's in disbelief—this disheveled little old guy pretending to be the great and powerful Wizard of Oz! She's on the verge of rage and tears.

She calls him a humbug, and he concedes.

Dorothy tells him he's a very bad man—but he corrects her. He says that he's no a bad man—just that he's a very bad Wizard.

Everyone's got blemishes.

Focus on people's positive qualities and you'll be surprised how often they want to shine.

When the Wizard says, "I'm a very good man—I'm just a very bad Wizard," I guess you can imagine how ticked off the whole crew is at hearing that!

There's a general mutiny, and everyone's as frightened as they are angry.

But they still intend to get what they came for.

The Scarecrow, the Wizard, and the Tin Man all ask about the things they've come for.

Now, here's where maybe the best dialogue in the whole film comes in: the Wizard seems to be back-pedaling. But actually the Wizard isn't back-pedaling at all.

He's dispensing pure, unadulterated wisdom.

And it's a beautiful thing to watch.

It's my favorite part of the film.

The Wizard explains that anyone can have a brain, that brains are very mediocre commodities. But deep thinkers have diplomas, he says. The Wizard takes one from a large black bag and bestows it upon the Scarecrow.

Then the Wizard turns to the Lion and explains that the Lion is a victim of disorganized thinking by believing that running away from danger is cowardly. Instead, the Wizard points out, running away from danger is wise.

But back where the Wizard comes from, they have men who are called heroes, and heroes have medals. He finds a convincing-looking triple-cross medal in his black bag and pins it on the Lion.

Kissing the Lion on both cheeks, the Wizard then turns his attention to the Tin Man. He takes a huge heart-shaped watch and chain out of his black bag and presents it to him.

Much merriment ensues, but then all of a sudden, the Scarecrow realizes something.

What about Dorothy? The Scarecrow, the Tin Man, and the Lion all want to know if the Wizard has a gift for Dorothy. Totally discouraged, Dorothy says she doesn't think there's anything in the Wizard's black bag for her.

But no. The Wizard says he realizes the only way for Dorothy to get back Kansas is for him to take her there himself.

Continuously Refine Your Plan

> **Wizard Wisdom:** *Write it down. Written goals have a way of transforming wishes into wants, can'ts into cans, dreams into plans, and plans into reality. Don't just think it—ink it. And when conditions change, modify your plan accordingly!*

Be flexible.

Make a list of things that you've been inflexible about and play "what if": what if you had been more flexible in that situation. How would the outcome have been different?

It's such a cliché that I even hate to say it, but *the only permanent thing in the universe is change.*

Therefore, be on the alert to constantly change your plan as you get new information, as you become wiser, as you work harder, and as conditions evolve.

So many people make a plan and work it so diligently that they forget they are in charge. Remember that you're calling the shots. For example, you plan on having a picnic, but then you learn that thunderstorms are on the way. Don't hesitate to go to a movie instead.

It always surprises me how stubborn people can be, when it's obvious that the best solution is to be flexible.

Time-Management Insights

Not too long ago, I went crazy trying to learn how to manage my time. I thought had too much to do and too little time to do it. At least I thought that was the case.

I tried managing my business, I tried selling, I tried speaking—all at one time—and it just didn't seem to work out. My day filled up too fast. I couldn't manage all of that stuff.

120

But guess what? I found out that I didn't have too much to do and that I didn't have too little time.

I figured out that if I took the time to put it all in order that I could make it all work.

I listened to some tapes about managing time, I read books, and I kept learning. I wanted to stay green all the time. I never wanted to get too comfortable, too complacent.

Somebody said, "If you're green you grow, if you're ripe you rot." Well, I wanted to stay green, so I had to keep growing. By learning and doing every day, I began to understand more about not only how I behave but—and this is important—how I behave in relation to time. What was really happening was that I was getting better at managing me.

For example, let's take the typical office desk.

Most people that I meet probably have a seriously cluttered desk. Lots of things are on their desks, and they keep moving piles around looking for something when the phone rings. They don't realize it, but by the end of a week, they have probably touched the same piece of paper twenty times, just moving it around.

Twenty years ago I attended a sales training course that focused on the skill of prioritizing. Boy, did that change things for the better!

That was when I first heard the phrase "the four Ds"—four words that absolutely will change how you manage the paperwork flowing to and from your desk.

This idea of the four Ds is so practical and so powerful in its simplicity that it will astound you. Let me tell you about the four Ds. I think you'll see what I mean.

Larry Wilson said if we're on two different sides of the mountain, and we start digging toward each other, and if we meet in the middle, we've dug one tunnel. If we don't meet, we dug two tunnels.

Four Ds for Better Self-Management

Take everything on your desk—and I mean everything on your desk—and stack it up into one big pile.

If the pile reaches up to the ceiling, start a new pile. Otherwise, stick with one big pile. Now, once everything is in that one pile, go to the first piece on the top of the pile.

Take it off the pile and look at it. Now, when you look at it, you have four Ds that you can apply to it.

The first thing you can do with it is "Do" it.

If it's a phone call to make, make the phone call. Right there and right then. Don't move a muscle until you've made that call. If the guy's not in or you don't get the information you need, then hang on to that paper until you've heard the rest of the four Ds, because then you'll know exactly what I want you to do with it.

If the first thing on that pile is a letter to write, then write the letter.

No matter what it might entail, do whatever task it is that piece of paper requires.

Some things you won't be able to do right away. If you can't do it immediately, go on to the second D. The action you want to take is to "Delay" it.

You may say, "I'm not going to do it today. I can't do it today. I have a good reason (not an excuse—a reason!) that I don't want to do it today. So, I'll put this task off for a future date."

To do this, you go to one of the file drawers that you have in your office and file that piece of paper for the appropriate date if it makes sense to do so. If you don't have the right kind of filing system, go out and get one of big calendars with a file for every day of the month and put that task off to a later date.

Let's assume you want to put it off until November. November 10. What you should do is put it in the November 9 slot, the day before.

122

Now, on November 9, when it comes, you'll pull out the file and complete the task.

The point of the second D—Delay—is if you're not going to do it now, and if you have a legitimate reason, you can put it off to a later date when it'll be more appropriate to deal with. It comes back to you automatically.

Now, let's say you know you won't be doing what is on the next piece of paper today, but you know you delaying it won't do any good. Then you must apply the next D to it. You have to "Delegate" it.

Have somebody else do it for you.

So, when that piece of paper comes off the top of the pile, you look at it and say, "I'm not going to do it today. I will not delay it today. But what I'll do is delegate it to somebody else."

Then give it to an associate, a secretary, a temp—whoever can handle it in a way that is more efficient and effective for you.

If I'm not going to do something, and I'm not going to delay it, and I don't think delegating it will do any good, do you know what the fourth D is? That's right. You must "Destroy" it. You must get rid of it.

If a piece of paper has been on your desk for months, and none of the first three Ds apply to it, do yourself a favor. Get rid of it. You're never going to do it anyway.

> *Insight from Oz:* Many people have a phobia about throwing things away. They think back to one or two incidents when they threw something away that someone later asked them for. Big deal. In 99 percent of these cases, the people are really exaggerating the memories of how serious a problem it was to not have that piece of paper. What do you think you are throwing away? The formula for the cure for cancer? Of course not. It's not critically important or you would have done something with it already. You'll probably throw away dozens of things that weigh you down just by their presence on your desk. If someday you have to make a call or two to get a copy of something you threw away, big deal. Your life will be so much less stressful for having thrown all of that distracting junk away in the first place that (maybe) having to track something down six months from now will be a piece of cake.

Back to that ceiling-high pile.

As you go through every piece of paper in that stack, you must decide, "Which of the four Ds will I do?"

There is not a fifth one. There are only four.

"I want to do it, I want to delay it, I want to delegate it, or if everything else fails, I'm going to destroy it, because I'm never going to do it anyway."

That's the conversation you ought be having with yourself.

I've found those four things valuable, because if I touch that piece of paper just once, I never have to come back to it. Ever.

Because of the fantastic organization that the four Ds gives me, I probably save myself a solid one hour a day using the four Ds. And I save a ton of aggravation, too.

That's six hours a week!

Times fifty-two weeks.

Three hundred and twelve hours a year!

That's practically eight full forty-hour weeks right there!

Eight weeks to do whatever I want with.

Go fishing?

Earn more money?

It doesn't matter, because my life is so much better, and all because of four simple words and an even simpler system.

Scheduling Appointments

On a daily basis, we have an interruption about every eight minutes in our offices.

And it is very difficult to stay on track and stay in focus with an interruption every eight minutes.

The telephone is probably *the* biggest interrupter. Now I pride myself in calling somebody back, either taking the call or calling back within an hour or two of any telephone call.

I probably get or make one hundred phone calls a day. Literally.

I make or take one hundred calls every day of my life. I'm not rude, but I don't wait. I make my own phone calls—nobody makes them for me.

If I have an appointment to sell you insurance on a Tuesday night next week, I guarantee that before I leave your home or office, I'll already have an appointment for the next time we have to meet. That way I save a phone call. I don't have to call back because we've already made a date. We know when we have to get back together, and I know what has to be done in order to prepare to get back together with you.

I set a time frame for the work to be performed.

Urgent, Important, and Everything Else

For Dorothy, every aspect of her sojourn in the land of Oz falls under the "Urgent" category. There is no time for taking breaks or stopping to smell the roses. It's full speed ahead the whole time.

But that is a fairy tale, and you live in the real world, where there are some urgent things, some important things, and then there's everything else.

I can't imagine how you can become a better salesperson at all without time control.

If you don't have some discipline in your life relative to how you deal with the twenty-four hours in a day, I don't see how you can sell anything to anybody.

Because the sales process requires discipline, and so do you.

But as I said earlier, I don't think you can manage time. What I suggest you shoot for is to find effective ways to manage *you*.

And I think your whole life will be much better if everything in it has some order.

I have a fantastic method—it works tremendously well for me—that I call "Urgent, Important, and Everything Else." I don't know exactly where it came from. It's been around—probably—for a hundred years.

To use Urgent, Important, and Everything Else, each day I make a list, and the list has three columns.

The first column is marked Urgent, the second one is Important, the third one is Everything Else. I haven't gone to sleep any night, 7 nights a week, 365 times a year, for the past twenty-five years without spending a minute or two reorganizing that list.

Now what exactly goes on that list?

Let's look at my list for today. In my Urgent column, there are only ten things that are Urgent, four that I rate as Important, and four things that I know must get done but that aren't burning my desk up.

Now, the Urgent things—they may not be earth-shattering issues, but in the scheme of things for me, I have made them my priorities. One of the items, for example, concerns something unrelated to business. Who cares? It's my life, and it's my Urgent, Important, and Everything Else list.

In my bedroom I have a TV, and my TV is controlled by one of those remote-control clickers, or channel changers.

Well, the clicker in my bedroom stopped working a couple of days ago. I pressed the clicker and it wouldn't do anything. Well then, I know I need a battery. The last thing you want to be is in your bedroom without a clicker, right? I don't want to have to get out of bed in the middle of the night to change the volume or the channel or shut the television off. So, on my Urgent list I wrote the word "battery."

Now, you might say, "How the heck can that be Urgent?

Easy. Because it's Urgent to me.

It's not on anybody else's list, I'm sure, but it's on mine.

Other things creep onto my list in the course of a day: call a certain client, finish a proposal, make a doctor's appointment, write a letter. What I do at night before I go to sleep is prioritize them.

I rank all the things on the Urgent column. I don't even bother with the Important or Everything Else columns.

I know that if I prioritize those top things on my Urgent list, tomorrow morning I'll wake up and start with number one, not going on to number two until I do one, and not doing three until I do two, and so on.

If I've done those most Urgent and Important things in my life that day, I'll sleep pretty well.

I've done all of those things that are Urgent and Important to me. And I do that every single day.

If you want to get something out of this information, no matter who you are, what you do, or where you are located, if you will just do this one ridiculously simple activity every day, your life will change, and you will prosper. You'll prosper in the ways you want to prosper.

You have to find one place to list everything. It can be in a daily planner or on a sheet of lined paper. It doesn't matter, as long as you stick to the system.

Mark it with the three columns and put down on that sheet everything that comes up that day. It is important that you don't have different sheets of paper, notebooks, tablets, computer screens, or index cards. Any one of those will do. More than one will undo the whole system. You'll never be able to track five different lists. Believe me, I've tried myself.

And every night before you go to sleep, prioritize them the one through ten. If you wake up the next morning, start with number one, and do the top-ten tasks in the order you set for yourself the night before, that alone will organize and prioritize your life. It will change the way you conduct your life because you will not have any more stress.

Everything will be done the way you want it. You'll have stress, but it will all be good stress, the kind of stress that you react to and then feel better about, not worse. And you know, we need some of that too.

Sometimes something that pops into my mind while I'm showering in the morning winds up on the list. How? Because the moment I'm dried off, as soon as I get out of the shower, I write it down on my list, which sits on my night table.

It might be to make a call to John Lallio, my attorney, or to let a client know his policy was approved, or to call Steve Brayden at New York Life to let him know that I will be out in California on Tuesday at 9 P.M. and that I want to get together when I'm out there—anything that clutters up my mind and can be better handled by getting it out of my head and onto the list. That's how it works best.

Remember, the things that make it to your list may not even make sense to anybody else. They don't have to. They are the most important things for me to do at this moment in my life. And if I do them, when I come home, I say, "Sue, I did everything I needed to do today, and I feel great."

That way I have a little breathing space, and I can move over to the Important things, the secondary things. And then some of them will suddenly seem like they ought to be the top priority, and I put them over in the Urgent column, and tomorrow, I'll nail them.

There will always be new Urgents, but that's not a problem. That's the beauty of the system.

New Urgencies, all the time—no problem.

Great Scene #11

Once again, Dorothy puts what is right before what she wants. By jumping out of the hot-air balloon before it lifts off to find Toto, she does herself the biggest favor possible. Because the balloon lifts off without her, she has to get home under her own power—the power of believing in herself. Had the Wizard taken her home, she wouldn't have learned that lesson—the most important lesson of all.

In the town square, Dorothy and the Wizard are standing in the basket of a striped hot-air balloon. The Scarecrow, the Tin Man, and the Lion are standing by, holding on to the balloon's ropes. On the balloon is painted: State Fair Omaha. Cheering throngs surround the scene. Toto, in Dorothy's arms, notices something and his ears prick up. Spotting a cat, he leaps forth and gives chase.

Dorothy and Scarecrow return to the platform as the balloon rises, slowly moving out of sight.

Dorothy can't believe what she is seeing.

She's seriously dejected. She believes that now she'll never be able to return to Kansas.

Little does Dorothy realize that Toto has just saved her once again!

Had she gotten back to Kansas under any power other than her own, she would have missed out on the most powerful lesson in the entire story: that she is capable of doing anything she sets her mind to.

But she's in tears, convinced she'll never get home. The Lion and the Scarecrow try to console her.

Suddenly, Glinda's bubble floats over the crowd. She's waving her wand in a friendly gesture to all the people.

Dorothy pleads for her help.

Glinda explains that Dorothy no longer needs her help. In fact, Dorothy is told that she has always had the power to go back to Kansas. The Scarecrow jumps in and, almost angrily, asks Glinda why she hasn't told this to Dorothy before now.

Because, Glinda says, Dorothy needed to learn that lesson for herself.

Even at the end of the story, when Toto jumps out of the balloon, Dorothy can still be seen racing after him.

Again.

She's dedicated to that dog.

The point is that by jumping out of the balloon after Toto, Dorothy eventually gets to see that she does not have to rely on the Wizard's power to get home, after all.

She's got all the skill and talent she needs.

If she had gone back with the Professor in the balloon, she would have been riding on someone else's coattails.

If she had gone with him, who knows? She might not even have gotten back to Kansas. Maybe it wouldn't have happened.

Once again, Toto zeroes right in.

Beautiful! What a story! What a story!

The Scarecrow and the Tin Man look to Dorothy to see her response to what Glinda has said. Dorothy is totally thrilled that she is almost on her way home to Kansas.

This is a benevolent universe, at least for those of us privileged to live in America, where most of us don't have to skip a meal or be sick without a doctor's care minutes away.

So it's reasonable to assume that the universe wants to help—but we just have to give it a chance.

We help the universe help us by putting forces of nature—human nature—to work.

Dreaming, planning, never letting up.
I can't say those words enough.

Dorothy emotionally says goodbye to everyone.
Dorothy hugs the Scarecrow.
Dorothy kisses him good-bye. She's crying.
Glinda asks Dorothy if she is ready. She nods "yes" and waves Toto's paw at everyone. Everyone waves back. Glinda tells Dorothy to close her eyes and tap her heels together three times.
Dorothy does it.
Glinda tells her to concentrate on the phrase, "There's no place like home."
Something powerful happens to Dorothy, because in a few seconds . . . she wakes up in familiar surroundings in Kansas.
She's in her own bed.

Get Past the Gatekeeper

Dorothy does it to get in to see the Wizard. You can do it to get in to see your prospects.

Secretaries, administrative assistants, junior executives—all of them want you to take "no" for an answer.

Don't do it.

The challenge is getting past the gatekeeper—the person standing between you and a face-to-face meeting with your prospect.

Concentrate on that and your sales will increase significantly.

The gatekeeper is the person whose job it is to keep you away from a sale.

And if you work it right, that gatekeeper can become your friend and your strongest ally, like a guard dog who takes a liking to you.

A Five-Year Plan

I look ahead five years at a time.

I break that period down into five one-year units, and then I break them down by the quarter, by the month, and finally, by the week.

The Time Design scheduling system makes organizing my time very simple. With it, I'm always in action. It's a moving, living planning tool. All the time.

I try not to think of today, other than my Urgent list.

I have to be in tomorrow. I'm always planning into tomorrow. I'm a tomorrow person.

Time Design is published in Sweden and is really nothing more than one of those day planners.

Whether you use a Daytimer or a Time Design or a Franklin Planner—it makes no difference. I've been using Time Design for ten years, and it works well for me. But this particular book works great for me. It's got a place for the daily plan, and I'm able to look at a whole year at a time on one sheet of paper, too. It helps me to be liquid when I'm doing my planning.

But that's just me. Any one of those books will do the job.

Do you have one? If not . . .

Take Action for Success!: *Stop reading this book and go out and get a comprehensive planning system!*

Words from the Wise
Valuable Insights about the Journey—from Successful People

I remember when I first started selling life insurance.

It seemed that the two most important parts of the day for most of the agents in that office was coffee break time in the morning and then coffee break time in the afternoon.

Except for one person—the highest-producing salesman in the agency.

One day, I approached that man and asked if he wanted to join us and the other agents for coffee.

"Ben," he said, "If I go for coffee in the morning, that winds up being about half an hour. Then there's another half an hour in the afternoon. That's an hour a day, six hours each week—practically a full day. That adds up to about one day a week, or fifty extra days each year! By skipping the coffee, I get an extra eight weeks of calls and contact over everyone else in the office. That's why I produce the most."

I walked away from the salesman for a moment, stuck my head into the coffee break room, and said, "See you guys later!"

—Ben Feldman

Discipline

Some people consider discipline a chore.
For me, it's a kind of order that sets me free to fly.

—Julie Andrews

Once you've got the dream and once you've laid it down, you've built a road map. The discipline is what needs to kick in once you press the Start button.

When it comes to self-discipline, Dorothy is a role model. Dorothy has natural discipline. Most of us don't. We have to develop it ounce by ounce. It's hard, like losing weight. But boy, when you look in the mirror and see how much discipline you've built, wow! There's nothing like it! A diet-center franchise used to advertise with this tag line: "Nothing tastes as good as thin feels!"

Well, no amount of lazy self-indulgence is as fun as genuine success feels!

Unfortunately, life is not one button you press that will last you the rest of your life. You have to keep pressing it all the time, over and over and over again.

Discipline. It's the motor in the back of the boat that powers your dreams and plans and goals. It's discipline that helps you keep that Start button in sight, and it's the schedule that reminds you that you have to keep pressing it over and over again.

Discipline is what keeps you from veering off the course you've plotted for yourself.

Discipline is what shows you where the Start button is.

Discipline is what allows you to press that button to make your system work.

Without discipline, none of this is possible. Discipline is what makes you go one step after the other without stopping, makes you relentless, makes you come back over and over again.

Think of the *Rocky* film in which Rocky fights the gigantic Russian. He goes to Siberia to train because he wants nothing to distract him from his mission of beating the Russian. He spends four months training. Every day, he just gets up and trains—trains to a point beyond what you expect from a human body. And the result? Well, when the fight first begins, it doesn't look too good for old Rocky Balboa, but after a while, all his effort and concentration pays off. Everything he has learned comes into play, and even though it is quite a challenge, he comes out the winner.

But none of that would have happened if he hadn't trained and trained and trained.

He wins because he is prepared.

Discipline is what makes him go, step by step, one piece at a time, small time, one thing after another, all small things, though. And again, that's the issue: discipline generally is not a matter of focusing attention on the big details.

It's attention to very, very small details—strung together—that as a whole packs a powerful punch. It is doing ordinary things—a lot of them—continuously, without getting up, never letting up.

That's how you make an ordinary person perform extraordinarily well.

Words from the Wise
Valuable Insights about the Journey—from Successful People

Not too long ago a thirty-year-old financial analyst was complaining to me over a period of months about her tendency to procrastinate. . . . I suggested that if she were to force herself to accomplish the unpleasant parts of her job during the first hour, she would then be free to enjoy the other six. It seemed to me, I said, that one hour of pain followed by six of pleasure was preferable to one hour of pleasure followed by six of pain. She agreed."

—M. Scott Peck, M.D.
The Road Less Traveled

Discipline Yourself

Discipline is a fundamental building block of success.

When space scientists use sophisticated telescopes to scan the heavens in their search for life elsewhere in the universe, they don't bother looking for the guys flying around in UFOs. It'd be a one-in-a-zillion chance they'd spot one. But what they do look for are the subtle signs that life *could* exist. They look for evidence of hydrogen and carbon, things that have to be present if life is going to exist.

Well, discipline is one of those building blocks. If you're not disciplined, you can't succeed. But if you are not particularly disciplined, don't worry. Because, unlike things you have no control over, discipline is something you can definitely learn.

I'm living proof of that.

What exactly is discipline? Well, I can answer that only as it applies to me, just as you can answer that only as it applies to you.

For me, discipline is a combination of commitment, courage, and the ability to delay gratification.

First, I have to make a commitment that I will see a particular plan through—from conception of the idea to its 100 percent completion.

Then I have to have the courage of that commitment, because when I wake up the morning after a great brainstorm, gravity will set in, and I'll have thousands of reasons why it won't work: I don't have the time, it wasn't a good idea to begin with, or I have an even better idea. The courage comes in when I stick to my original plan.

And the delayed-gratification part is tough. It's always a beautiful day, and I'd like to be outside enjoying it. There is always something more fun to do. But there's nothing more important than doing what I promised myself I would do.

I have a friend who's a recovering alcoholic. He always says that there are a million *excuses* to pick up a drink—but no good *reasons*.

It's the same with work and discipline. There are many excuses to not do what you have promised you'd do—but not one good reason.

The fact of the matter is that there are certain things you have to do to get to where you want to be, and while you are sitting at you desk or out on the road doing them, you are not going to be at the movies, on the golf course, or reading a book. You are going to be working. And unless you do what needs to be done, and do it with dedication, you will never get what you want out of life. And then suddenly when you're sixty or seventy or eighty, you'll be scratching your head and wondering why so many people with less talent than you were able to make it. And you'll be right: many of them did have less natural talent than you, but they had something else that more than made up for it—discipline.

They had the commitment, the courage, and the ability to delay gratification.

You can't change things if you keep doing what you've always been doing. If you don't do things differently than how you already do them, you'll get nothing different from what you've been getting.

Know You Want the Ace of Hearts

By being disciplined, I accomplish maximum productivity, and I do it in less time then I'd have spent without discipline. It comes by knowing what I want to do in the first place.

If I asked you how many cards there are in a deck of cards, what would you tell me?

Fifty-two.

If I asked you how many suits there are, what would you tell me?

Hearts, diamonds, clubs, spades.

How many colors are in the deck?

Red and black.

If I said to you, "What are the chances you will pick the ace of hearts out of this entire deck?"

"One out of fifty-two," you'd say.

But you'd be wrong. There is a 100 percent chance you will pick the ace of hearts out of all the cards.

How can that be?

Easy! Because *I already know what I want to do* with the deck of cards. I already have my plan, and now I just have to use a minute amount of discipline—in this case, it is nothing more than actually carrying out the card trick—to real my goal.

"Here are fifty-two cards," I say. "Pick any one, look at it, and then put it back into the deck and tell me its color.

So you pick a card, put it back, and tell me it's black.

"Ah, ha!" I say. "Black! Well, then I'll just remove all the black cards."

Then I look through the deck and remove every black card.

I shuffle the rest—they are all hearts and diamonds, of course—return them to you, and tell you to pick a card, look at it, and while still holding on to it, tell me its suit.

You do it and tell me, "Hearts."

"Ah, ha!" I say. "Hearts! OK, then, hang on to that card while I get rid of all the diamonds. I then go through the deck, remove all the diamonds, and take the one card you are holding. I put all the cards in order—from deuce to ace—but I don't show you. I put them face down on a table in three groups. Two-three-four-five-six, then seven-eight-nine-ten, and the last group Jack-Queen-King-Ace.

"Point to any group," I tell you.

Remember, I know which cards are in which group face down on the table.

If you point to the group with the ace of hearts in it, I say "Ah-ha!" and scoop up all the rest. But if you point to a group that doesn't have the ace of hearts in it, I'll scoop up that pile and discard it.

Then I'll do it again until only the pile with the ace of hearts in it remains.

"Now," I'll say, "point to any one of those four remaining cards." If I get lucky, and you point to the one that is the ace of hearts, I'll shout, "You're darn right!" and I'll jubilantly flip it over with a great flourish and shake your hand!

If, however, you point to one of the three cards that is not the ace of hearts, I'll say, "Excellent!" and sweep it away into the discard pile.

I'll then arrange the three remaining cards, and name them—maybe something like Vanilla, Chocolate, and Strawberry—and tell you to pick a flavor. If you pick the one that's the ace of hearts, I'll say, "Gee, you really do like Strawberry!" and hand you the ace of hearts. But if you point to any card other than the ace of hearts, I'll just say, "Great!" and sweep that card into the discard pile.

You don't object because you're not quite sure of what the rules are. I never told you what I would do with the cards you pick, so, since I seem so pleased and everything keeps moving along, the game seems as if it's going according to plan—and it is!

My plan!

I knew you were going to pick the ace of hearts.

Now the reason I knew that is because by the way I questioned you, I knew where I wanted to go before I began.

Let me tell you how I did that.

By questioning you and by knowing where I wanted to go in the first place, I was going to leave you with the ace of hearts, no matter what you directed me to do. No matter how you answered my questions, I was going to leave you with the ace of hearts.

Well, I think that is what life is all about. Knowing that you want the ace of hearts in the first place and conducting your life accordingly along the way, but by right questioning, right positioning, right activity. No matter what happens, you are shooting for the ace of hearts.

Everybody gets his heart's desire. Everyone wins, and nobody loses.

Now that's what I do all the time. You may call that manipulation, but I call it proper planning.

No matter what obstacle Dorothy faces, it doesn't matter. It's Kansas City, Kansas City, here she comes!

Never Let Up

*No Matter How Difficult Your Yellow
Brick Road Becomes, Keep Moving Forward*

Replay in your mind the scene of Dorothy being held captive by the Wicked Witch in her castle. Many people wouldn't be able to fight such overwhelming odds: superior strength, hundreds of flying monkey warriors, and a nasty array of evil spells.

But Dorothy does. Her goal is clear. She just keeps hammering at it.

You may sometimes find yourself in a tough, tough situation that you feel is just not worth fighting.

But before you give up, ask yourself, "What's not worth it?"

All the hassles, the headaches, the staying late, the doing things you don't feel like doing.

When I occasionally start to feel that way, I look myself in the mirror and say, "So what!" I remind myself that my temporary frustrations are just that—temporary—and they are usually telling me something is out of balance. I analyze what's really bothering me, and I try to make the adjustment. Do you know how many potentially extraordinary people take those passing frustrations to heart—*and then give up on their plans on the basis of normal, temporary feelings?*

Too many!

I ask myself, "Is my goal worth it? Is the end result worth it?" And the answer is always the same: *It sure is worth it!*

Some of the pieces along the way may be not worth it, I admit. But you can't pick and choose. If there are ten tasks associated with what you are trying to accomplish, maybe three of the ten parts really stink. Although difficult and uncomfortable for you, they are things you believe you have to do yourself. So you do them. But the ten parts together are really exciting. So, what do you do? You do all ten—the seven parts you like and three parts you don't. You do them all. What does what you enjoy have to do with anything?

You can't stop. Because if you miss the three things, you also miss the seven. You have to see all ten as part of a whole, part of another step toward whatever goal you've established. That's delaying the gratification. It's like saving the dessert for last.

Hey, who am I kidding? Sometimes it's worse than that. Maybe there are seven things that stink and only three that you like. Or maybe there are nine things that stink and one you like, but if those ten, all together, make it work, then never let up.

You will get what you want.

Impossible Obstacles

Just say "No!"
—Drug-abuse prevention slogan

Years ago, when I had cancer in my left eye, the prescribed radiation treatments had a very serious side effect on my body.

Radiation is powerful medicine, of course. It has to be—that's the point of it. But the side effects don't occur during the actual treatment. They kick in later.

I had forty-six consecutive days of radiation, after which the doctors give me a month's break, and then I had forty-six more days.

Believe me, that radiation had a debilitating impact, but, like it or not, I didn't have a choice. It was a life-or-death situation. Literally.

About two months after the treatment ended, it started to affect my body. My energy level dropped down to almost nothing. It was as if somebody had unscrewed my big toe and all of my energy had drained right out.

I had to find a way to get it back. I had to replenish it and keep it inside me. If I hadn't, I would have wound up just sitting there. I was really exhausted most of the time.

I had two choices. One was to just give into it, lie down, and take a nap until it passed—which might have been four or five months—or I could have gone the other way and marshaled all of my strength, all of my thoughts, all of my energy, to focus on my goals. I had to work even harder than I used to work.

You might say to yourself, "Well, how's that possible? How can somebody go from already working hard, having all this debilitating radiation that knocks you down, and then go out and work twice as hard?"

The answer is simple. I had to do it.

It's almost like the stories you've probably heard about the 115-pound guy who finds his best friend trapped under an overturned truck. The little guy somehow lifts the whole truck up by himself, and then he uses his other hand to drag his buddy out. It's almost an impossibility. A guy can't lift a truck up by himself—unless he has to.

It was almost an impossibility, but I had to get myself together and instead of just working only very hard—which is my usual speed—I worked extra very hard. And here's an amazing thing: after a while, I forgot that I was exhausted. I just didn't notice it anymore. My perception of it went away. The word "tired" just wasn't in my vocabulary. I guess I was pushing so hard that I told my body, "Hey, no matter how tired you think you are, you're not."

Maybe that sounds kind of unlikely, but the fact is that I simply wouldn't give in to the weariness. And it was there, believe me. It was like a heavy, soggy woolen blanket draped over me twenty-four hours a day. But I kept doing what I had to do, and I got so busy I forgot that I was tired.

That's the truth.

Every once in a while, I have to admit, the fatigue sneaked up on me when I wasn't looking. Hit me like a freight train. I didn't even have a chance to wrestle with it. Several times it knocked me down so hard that I couldn't move for a day. One day, maybe two. But that was it. I got back up again and I worked harder, and the harder I worked, of course, the luckier I got. The more I worked hard, the more I forgot about my problems. I don't doubt that working hard had something to do with how wonderful my recovery was.

I kept working and working and working until I worked through it all—the fatigue, the exhaustion, the complete lack of energy.

I never let up. Then one morning I woke up, looked around, and found that I had made it through and had come out on the sunny side of the tunnel.

Know Your Enemy!

First, know your enemy! When you find yourself confronted with a seemingly impossible obstacle, get out a sheet of paper (or turn on your computer) and create a dossier on the problem. If you want, you can pretend you are a government agent assigned to solve the problem, and you have to do all the background work to get the investigation rolling. Get all the facts organized. Write down everything you know about the problem: its source, its impact on you, its impact on others. Describe the worse-case scenario. Make a note of how it happened. Make a note about what will happen if the problem is not solved.

Call in the experts. Who has expertise on the kind of problem confronting you? Consult with those who know or with friends or associates who have been through similar situations. Use your brain as well as your ears to listen to everyone who has an idea, but use your gut to decide the best course of action.

Get a clear mental picture of what the situation will look like once you find a way to solve it. Obviously, there is quite a gap between your existing problem and a satisfactory solution.

Break the problem down into smaller, more manageable hurdles and tackle the easiest ones first. Why the easiest first, when I normally suggest getting the toughest challenges out of the way sooner rather than later? Well, because, when overwhelmed with a serious problem, a few early successes in working on a solution can give you a tremendous start and have you feeling that, "Hey, this bear really can be wrestled into submission!"

Become an Expert at Patience and Perseverance, or Watching the Cat

One summer afternoon I went to see a reluctant prospect. I was getting frustrated by his hemming and hawing.

No matter how much you think being patient is worth, I guarantee it that you are underestimating its value.

Have you ever watched a cat sitting near a birdfeeder? During the course of this meeting, I had the chance to glance out into a yard at one throughout the afternoon. That cat sat there for hours, all afternoon—just to catch that one robin that wasn't paying attention.

That cat sat there for maybe four, five, or six hours before it scored. But on the way home with its prize in its mouth, that cat wasn't fretting over how much time it had waited. It was ecstatic that it got what it wanted. That cat reinforced what I know about patience.

And by the way, even though it took all day, I did make the sale.

Perhaps there is only one cardinal sin: impatience! *Because of impatience we were driven out of paradise, and because of impatience we cannot return.*
—W. H. Auden

Insight from Oz: Go for progress, not perfection. When people believe that finding a 100 percent solution to a particular problem is unlikely, they often don't even bother to begin looking. It is the rare problem that cannot be improved one way or the other.

Goal Obstacles

There will always be lions and tigers and bears—oh my!—there will always be obstacles put in your path, but if there is no good logical or emotional reason for you to stop the project, don't stop it.

And be tough on yourself.

So many times in the past, before I taught myself how to be successful, I would be confronted by a problem and then say, "Well, here's a tough problem. I'd better give up on it and move on to something else, something easier."

I wasn't looking deeper into the situation. I'd have an emotional reaction: "Uh-oh! A big problem." And I'd take off.

Since then, I've learned that if you put a big, bright spotlight on something and examine it, most of the time it will turn out to be like the Wizard of Oz: really just a little fellow behind a curtain trying to scare the heck out of you.

What I am recommending is to *always peek behind the curtain!*

First, determine if an obstacle is logical or emotional.

If it is emotional, then try to figure out what the underlying problem is.

On the other hand, if the reason you need to abort a project is logical or practical, try this: Tell yourself that it is just impossible to get out of and you have to figure out the next-best thing to do. Now, even though you know full well that you can quit the project, you'll be surprised what you'll come up with when you put your talent and imagination into solving the problem. If you are like me, you've already learned how talented and imaginative you can be when it comes to getting out of doing something. Now, try putting that same energy into finding a solution.

More Trade Secrets

Cold Calls vs. Referrals

It's obvious that a referral is a thousand times better than a cold call.

And although most salespeople know it, they don't act like they believe it!

They don't knock themselves out getting referrals.

It's important that people buy into you. It is so much easier to make that first sale and have someone buy into you if you come by way of a referral.

I try to get away from the cold calls. The gatekeeper is looking for you to call.

We have a telemarketing system in my agency that succeeds in getting us in to see people, but ten of those leads aren't half as good as one decent referral. When that one good referral is set up, that gatekeeper is waiting to see you instead of waiting to pounce on you.

"Oh, we were expecting your call! Thanks for coming, Sid. Come on in."

Via a referral, the gatekeeper becomes part of the solution rather than staying part of the problem, and your prospect is already warmed up before you even sit down.

"I'm Going to Find a Way to Get to Kansas"— Keeping Promises to Yourself

I recently had a speaking engagement in Providence, Rhode Island. I was the luncheon speaker scheduled for 1 P.M. I was to be on for an hour and a quarter. The meeting organizers were paying me a nice speaking fee, and I had to be there in time for that meeting.

For one reason or another, I couldn't go to Providence the night before. I got up the morning of the speech and went to the Philadelphia airport for a 6:30 A.M. flight that would get me to Providence by 7:30 A.M.

I arranged the flight so that I would be at the location at 8 A.M. and have from 8 A.M. to 1 A.M. to schmooze with the attendees. And even if the plane was an hour or two late—even though that was unlikely—I'd still be there in plenty of time.

Anyway, I was booked on a U.S. Air flight, so I went to the U.S. Air counter only to learn that the flight's been canceled because of fog.

Not U.S. Air's fault. Not my fault. No one's fault.

But I still had a commitment to keep.

Unanxious, I said, "OK, fine. The flight's canceled due to fog. I understand that. How else can I get there? I absolutely have to Rhode Island—and quickly."

"Well," the counter guy said, "we have another flight through Boston. We can fly you out there through Boston, from there to Boston, and then you can drive to Providence. It's about an hour-and-a-half ride."

I cheered up quickly.

"Great! What time does that flight leave?" I asked.

"It leaves in about forty minutes, Mr. Friedman. Let me make a phone call for you."

The guy called the counter. For some reason, because of mechanical failure or fog, that Boston flight was not taking off after all.

"This can't possibly be happening to me," I said. "Find me any other flight on any airline in North America that'll go from Philadelphia to Providence today and can get me there by 1 P.M.!"

A supervisor then came over and tried to help.

"Well, you're lucky," she said. "There's a Newark, New Jersey, flight. We'll fly you here to Newark and take you from Newark up to there. Mr. Friedman, we'll call that gate."

Great! Everything'll work out! I thought.

They called the gate for the Newark flight, but no one answered. They called and called and let it ring and ring. The gate for Newark had been abandoned. Nobody was there. That flight also had been canceled because of some problem or another.

As a result, I had no way to get to Providence. They checked the computer to find that there were simply no flights that were going to meet my schedule.

The clock struck 10:30. After spending all this time trying to make arrangements to get there, I didn't know what to do because I didn't have the heart to call these people and tell them I couldn't make it.

The guy who was supposed to pick me up at the airport at 8 A.M. had already heard from me that I wasn't going to make my flight but that I'd page him every hour on the hour to keep him abreast of my schedule.

During my latest call I could tell that he was beginning to panic. I was the only speaker of the day. People had paid to come to that luncheon to hear Sid Friedman speak, and Sid Friedman was still standing around in Philadelphia.

By then I was feeling like I had a real problem. I lost my opportunity to drive—it was a physical impossibility because the ride would take six hours. I didn't know what to do.

I decided to call U.S. Air to hire me a private plane.

"Mr. Friedman, we can't," the airline said. "It's not our responsibility to get you a private plane."

"That's right," I said, "but it was your responsibility to get me up in the air so I could get there."

To make a long story short, they couldn't help me get a private plane.

Scratching my head, I remembered that Atlantic Aviation, a private airline company, was based at Philadelphia International airport. I called them for a plane.

"Sorry, Mr. Friedman. We haven't got a single plane in the area to get you there in time. It's an hour-and-a-half flight."

"That's not an answer I can hear. Find me an airplane," I said.

Well, in a few minutes, they found one man who had a plane, a light twin, who said, "For $1,500, I'll fly you there and fly you home. But I definitely can't leave until 12:30. And it's an hour-and-a-half ride to Providence."

"Wait a minute," I said.. "You don't understand. I have to be there for a speech at 1 P.M."

"I'll tell you what I'll do," he said. "I can stop another flight that's scheduled and send a smaller plane. But I'll incur additional costs to do it that way. So, instead of costing you $1,500, it's going to cost you $2,200. Do you want it?"

"Sold!" I said. "How quick can you be here?"

He was there in ten minutes, we boarded the plane, and I landed at the airport at 12:10. It took twenty-five minutes to drive to the meeting. Then I had to set up the stuff I use when I make my presentations.

At exactly two minutes to 1 P.M., the announcer tapped me on the shoulder and said, "Are you ready?"

"Sure."

And I made my speech for an hour and a quarter.

I want you to know that the fee for speaking that day was less than the $2,200 it cost me to get there. So, I didn't go through all of that do it for the money. I did it because I promised those guys in Providence—and I promised myself—that I'd be there.

It turned out that the speech that day was a smash hit. I started out by telling the story about the airline trouble to the audience, and I got a standing ovation.

The point of the story is that I had made a promise. And you know my principle: "Promise a lot—and deliver even more!"

But, more importantly, I had a goal, and even though I had a serious challenge, at least I knew where I was going.

I knew where I was—in Philadelphia. And I knew where I had to be—in Providence. And no matter what happened, I had to get there.

I gave my word. Keeping my word is what drives my whole life. And I'm trying to get to you to adopt that philosophy and let it drive your whole life.

Maybe I'm fanatic about it, and maybe you won't be as fanatical as I am. But the fact is that when you make a promise, the most important promise you make is really to yourself. This promise wasn't made to the folks in Providence; the promise was really made to me.

I think that if I hadn't have done all that I did to get myself to Providence, I wouldn't have felt good about myself.

Insight from Oz: There are at least two "you"s. And the promises you make to the ambitious "you" in bed at night have to be kept for the less ambitious "you" who is in your bed when you wake up the next morning.

Words from the Wise
Valuable Insights about the Journey—from Successful People

I have a relentless drive to reach any goals I set for myself, and today I operate three successful businesses.

I never let myself get off course. No matter what comes up, I just charge through.

My advice is simple: be direct, be honest, and follow up and follow up and follow up and follow up. After that, follow up some more.

If someone calls me and tells me they are interested in a car, I keep that person's name on a sheet of paper until forever—until they buy or until they die.

Following up is the key. Just tell people the way it is. No one I know has time for b.s. today. Back up any sales with solid information.

The various crossroads in my life have taught me that just sticking to hard tasks is the key. That's what brings you through it. Nothing good lasts forever, and same with bad. That won't last forever, either.

I reached a turning point in my early thirties—I'm fifty-three now—when I worked for a man who taught me self-discipline. He taught me that there is no shortcut to success. That man taught me to stick with one thing, hard work, and discipline myself. One of the great things I learned from him is that the grass is *not* greener. It only looks that way.

—Billy Stamps

How to Find Your Own Yellow Brick Road

If you really want to be successful, and if you know where you are now before you go any farther, and you dream in color, and you decide to make your dream a reality, and you know how to manage yourself so you take advantage of the time you have, and you develop some good habits of self-discipline, and you prepare your mind with inside ideas and trade secrets, and you learn to never let up, *then you absolutely have to be moving full speed ahead.*

You are going as fast as you can go.

All of this adds up to developing the road map for the trip you want to go on. You are developing the picture of what's going to be done.

This process is akin to the American Automobile Association's Triptik.

This is the map that takes you from where you are now to where you want to go. So all this dreaming, all this never letting up, is all the same thing: it is never letting go of this map.

The map will get you there. Put everything into your map and stick with it.

Mark Twain refuted the logic that says, "Never put all your eggs in one basket." He said, "Put all your eggs in one basket—*but watch that basket!*"

You need to create a plan—the pages of the Triptik that will get you from where you are to where you want to go.

Insight from Oz: *Commit your plan to paper or it will never happen. Make it a living document that you refer to, modify, and update.*

Your plan—it's never going to work if it exists just in your head.

You have to reduce it to writing so you can refer to it, because what's in your head will fall out. So you have to put it on paper.

148

For example, let's say I'm writing a book that has ten sections.

I put a sheet of paper for each of the ten sections together in my planner. And every time I think of something, I see where it fits in the ten sections and jot it down. Over the months, without doing much more than random thinking on the book, I look into my notebook and see that I've got about 80 percent of the book very thoroughly thought out. *There is no way I could have made that much progress without the benefit of capturing those ideas and putting them on paper.* If you think you have a good memory, answer this question: What did you have for lunch the day before yesterday? At the moment you were eating that lunch, it was important and had all of your concentration. Today, you may not even remember where you ate, let alone what you ate. Time fades things, especially ideas!

When I make a note about my book, I can look back and be confident about the quality of those sections, because I thought about them carefully. Sure, maybe they'll change as I get deeper into the process, but maybe they won't. But I know one thing: I'm pretty close, and I can move ahead knowing I'm on the right road.

These ideas occur—not when I want them, but when they pop up.

More Trade Secrets

The "Discovery" Sales Process

At my agency, we spend about 80 percent of our sales training time on developing "discovery" skills. What are the problems your potential client might have that would be solved by the purchase of your product?

A salesman used to work out of a book and say, "I've got a solution here. Do you have a problem?"

And now we are trying to teach them to forget about the problem. First, conduct the discovery, find out the problem, and then let your prospects help you solve that problem for them.

One of the most powerful tools you can have is the ability to do good discovery work. It will increase your close rate dramatically.

Make a Plan, Achieve a Goal

1. Focus on a vision.

This was something Dorothy did instinctively. Once you get a goal, it becomes easier to tune out all the information that doesn't relate to your goal. Your vision becomes a source of inspiration, but the fact is, you have to have that dream first, and as I keep saying, you have to dream it vividly.

2. Define the purpose of the mission.

Look at the project or goal with the end in mind. Each and every day you must decide to do things that will motivate you and get you closer to that vision.

Because once you align your actions, you can then just make sure that what you're doing every day gets you closer to the thing you want. It makes it easier to rule out everything else, too.

It's like having a hot knife to cut through a stick of butter.

3. Measure your progress.

To make sure you're on that track, find a way to measure how well you are faring in moving along toward your goal. Create a system you can stick to for constant measuring. It doesn't matter if it's every hour, every day, every week, or even once a decade—as long as the measurement system is appropriate for whatever it is you are working on.

Insight from Oz: Break the steps down into bite-size pieces.

If you're shooting for an annual sales goal of $100,000, that goal might look very difficult. However, if you break it down by the month, you get down to $8,133 a month. That's the same $100,000, but it seems like it's a bite-size piece. And if that's too heavy, you might go by the week and say, "I can't do that much, but I can do $2,000 a week."

And if that's too much, maybe ask yourself how many sales you'd have to make every week to get there? And if you add up the pieces of the day, the week, the month—all of a sudden a year comes to fruition.

Falling behind Your Goals

Let's assume that you miss a week and you fall behind your goal.

You might be tempted to say, "Well, instead of doing one hundred, I'll do ninety-eight this year."

Wrong.

What you need to do is to find a way to get back on track and pick up that $2,000 the following week.

> **Insight from Oz:** *It's a cinch by the inch, hard by the yard. If you miss a day or a week or even a month, so what? Get right back on track. It's like that business about trying to get past a wall. Either you go around it, above it, or under it. If you have to, you go through it. But you get yourself past it, no matter what.*

More Trade Secrets

Follow-Up after Your Client Meeting

When I leave a sales appointment, I get in my car. I have a telephone in the car, and I call a voice-mail box back at my office.

I dictate what I call "notes to the file"—everything that went on in that interview, completely, even down to the small details like "the client had a cold" or "there was something going on in his plant that particular day." That way, when I look at the file again, I can tune back to the emotions of the situation.

And what I do when I finish the notes to the file is give instructions to the staff on who's got to do what to prepare me for the next appointment. The staff knows when it is, and they do the workup, and everyone knows what's expected and what just happened at the appointment.

I also do something unique.

I have the notes in the voice-mail file typed up immediately so that they are there when I get back into the office. My secretary knows that I've been dictating them in my car because a light comes on at her desk. She gets to them immediately, so that when I get back, the notes are on my desk.

I say to the client—before I leave him at that appointment—"Listen, I want to be sure that I heard what you said. As a matter of fact, I want to be so sure I heard what you said before I go to work on the problem that I'm going to dictate my notes to a voice-mail file. And when I get to my office, I'm going to look at them. If they sound correct, I'm going to Federal Express them to you with a little red pencil inside the envelope. I'd fax it, but I want you to have this little red pencil. When you get it, I want you to look the notes over and make sure that what I heard you say was, in fact, what you said—that we understand each other. And as soon as you get it, there will be another envelope that is Federal Express, already paid for. Review the notes and send it right back to me. That way I'll know what you said was what I heard."

Now when I get this back, it lets me know he's reviewed the notes to the file and that I've heard the right information. And now I can go to work in handling the problems that I see out of the facts.

And when I see him again, the first thing we do is pull out the notes to the file, with his red comments on them, and I ask him to please read it back aloud to me.

By doing that, we nail down that I understood what he said.

And then I ask him, "Are those facts still the same? Has anything changed?"

Once he's said that the facts are still the same, I know I am on the right track.

By the way, I make two or three mistakes on purpose. I will misquote an age of a child, for example, knowing full well that she's not five, but fifteen. Now he has a chance to check and change and be a part of the process. I'm getting him involved from the very beginning.

He has to change something. If he didn't change something, I know he didn't read it. And if he sends it back to me, he's going to have read it. If he sends it back to me, he's going to buy. Because as you and I well know, 90 percent of the sale is made in the discovery—not in close.

And if you do the discovery process and you ask the right questions up front, you never have to worry about a close. It can be assumed, because we'll have dug one tunnel instead of two.

What does that mean?

Larry Wilson once said that if we're on two different sides of the mountain digging toward each other, if we meet in the middle, we've dug one tunnel. If we don't meet, we dug two tunnels.

I've never forgotten that. We always have to meet in the middle. If we don't meet in the middle, there's no sale. I don't care how hard you close—no matter how cute a close you have—if you don't do the right discovery, you will never discover the problem. And then there's no chance for a solution.

When you slip, you slip.

It happens every day.

You have to make up that $2,000. Now, you can make it up all in one fell swoop the following week, or you can break the $2,000 up into smaller pieces and make them up over time.

We all need to tune in to what we want to accomplish and find a way to concentrate on it, never taking our minds off it.

In other words, is what I'm doing now helping me to get closer to my goal? Is what I'm doing at this very moment in time going to get me to stay on my track? Do I have landmarks along the way so I know I'm going correctly?

As long as you keep an eye out for the landmarks, you'll make up any deficiencies you have.

If you keep going and going and going and doing what you said, you'll get to where you want to be.

More Trade Secrets

"I Don't Know"

Don't be afraid to say, "I don't know!"

The concept of promising much and delivering more is very important.

If you tell the prospect, "I don't have the answer to that question, but I have a whole army of people back in my office who can get that answer for me and I'll get back to you in twenty-four hours. Is that satisfactory?" I guarantee you'll earn ten times more respect than if you fake an answer.

People will understand that you care, and when you do call back with the information, that's another opportunity to develop that relationship and build your credibility.

Goal Setting and Developing a Mind-Set for Success

"I Have Three Words for You: Kansas, Kansas, Kansas!"

Developing a way of thinking that automatically guides you to success is a critical step in finding what you set out to find. The fundamentals are simple. I want you to see them again and again in everything you do. I can only repeat them a few times here, but I am counting on you to find a way to remind yourself of them constantly.

1. Focus on a vision.
2. Define your purpose or mission.
3. Measure the goals. . . .
4. Develop a new mind-set for success.

The mind-set for success is different than dreaming. It's a very important step. You have to be able to picture yourself reaching your goal.

That's what I mean by "beginning with the end in mind."

Can you see yourself in victory? Can you see what it looks like at the end?

Can you see yourself accomplishing and attaining that goal of $100,000 this year?

Can you see yourself having problems during the course of the year and overcoming them as you go along? Can you see yourself overcoming adversity—no matter what—to get to the end result?

You're not going to get the end result unless you can do that, unless you can absolutely see the end.

There are many clients who say no to me. And they say no plenty of times. As a matter of fact, I look forward to noes because I can't get those yeses until I get a certain amount of noes. The noes give me something to sink my teeth into. If a client isn't objecting to what I'm saying, then he or she isn't listening. I'm not having a conversation—I'm making a speech!

So you can say that I actually look forward to noes to get them out of the way.

Not everybody is going to say yes, no matter what I do. No matter who you are, there's no salesperson in the world that gets yes all the time. There will be a certain amount of noes. Plenty of noes!

So the trick for me is to get those noes going. I get the one yes in the middle of a bunch of noes. I just don't know which no will be the first to turn into a yes.

It may sound off base, but it is true that I learn more from mistakes than I learn from successes. Of course, the successes pay better in cash, but the mistakes pay better—much better—in wisdom.

You've heard about Anthony Hopkins, who played Dr. Hannibal Lecter in *The Silence of the Lambs*? Well, until he did that role, he wasn't very well known, despite being about sixty years old at the time. He went on to win an Academy award for that role. Well, an interviewer was talking with him and said, "Wow! That one movie made you an overnight success!"

And Hopkins said something like, "Yeah sure! It took me forty years to become an overnight success!"

Each time you have a little success—no matter how inconsequential—it sets you up for doing better in the future.

What you learn in those forty years adds up.

All those noes, all those negatives, all that aggravation, all that down stuff sets up all the wonderful things that happen today.

That's what I mean when I talk about developing a mind-set.

5. Think in pictures or models—but not words.

You can't just tell yourself you're going to be successful. You have to come up with little anecdotes in your mind, little ideas in your brain that show you what that success is going to feel like. What trappings will you have by getting the success?

Just saying you'll make $100,000 is not satisfactory. What will you do with the $100,000? How will you feel about your journey once you've arrive at where you wanted to go? What does the $100,000 represent?

It may represent a new house, maybe a vacation, maybe some new clothes, maybe a car, or maybe just a bigger bank account balance. Whatever it means, it means something to you that you can conjure up in an image—rather than just the words "I want to make a 100 grand."

That's not enough; it won't work.

6. Create a reward system for yourself. As you do something good, give yourself a reward.

Assuming that for the week—in that example of $100,000—you did your $2,000 and you feel very comfortable because it happened by Thursday, even though you had until Sunday to make it.

Maybe the reward you'll set is that one night that week you may go out to dinner when normally you wouldn't have gone out—because you'd be working. Treating yourself to a special meal is just one way of rewarding yourself.

And maybe if you reach your goal by Wednesday instead of by Sunday or by Thursday, you'll give yourself a bottle of cologne or brand-new shirt. Maybe you'll take some of that time and do a good deed—visit some lonely person or do something that normally turns you off, even though you know it's a good thing to do. That way, you take a little success, and make it a bigger one, a more significant one.

When you achieve your goal earlier than you expected, make sure to tell yourself, "Good boy!"

When you do something well, don't hesitate to indulge yourself.

All successful people have their own personal reward system. They may keep it to themselves, but I'll bet anything that they all have one.

Wizard Wisdom: Look at these steps again and plant them in your mind:

- *get a vision*
- *define that purpose or mission*
- *measure your goals*
- *develop a new mind-set for success*
- *think in pictures or in models, not in words*
- *create your own reward system*

All of these things can help you get where you want to go, if you know what you want, and I think there's a power in that enthusiasm that comes up.

Early Enthusiasm

From the very start, Dorothy knows what her game plan is.

It was the same with me. When I first came to Phoenix Home Life thirty years ago, I would leave home very early in the morning and come home late at night.

The only way I'd get to see Sue, my brand-new wife of about a year, was for her to stay up late at night. But she worked all day. In order to stay up late at night, when she came home from work, she would cook dinner and then take a nap. When I'd come home about midnight, we'd have dinner for an hour and get a chance to talk to each other. That went on for about a year.

We eventually got an opportunity to move to Philadelphia from New York. Although my extensive traveling stopped, the kind of work I was doing still kept me on the job for many hours. Sue and I both knew, instinctively, that without that kind of dedication, I just wouldn't be able to succeed. We both agreed it was worth it, and it turned out we were right.

I must tell you that when I first started my insurance agency some thirty years ago, the silence in the office was deafening.

When I first got here, I looked at the personnel and realized that, although there were twenty-six bodies there, there were only three agents who could really sell insurance. The other twenty-three people were just taking up space and time.

I came into the agency not knowing a whole bunch about management, but I did know something about the sales process. However, I was really an unconscious competent. I was doing it right, but I had no idea how or why I was doing it right.

So I had to work pretty hard. I came to the agency and I looked over all the records and I spent the first thirty to forty days locked up in a room they called my office. It was really a plain, wooden desk—not much more than a box—and I had lots of records from the previous ten years.

I looked over all the records, and when I came out of the office, I knew that twenty-three of those twenty-six guys had to go.

They collectively weren't doing $5,000 in commissions a month. The bulk of the commissions were being done by three people, and that was stinky too, but you can only imagine how stinky the rest of it was.

So I gave termination notices to all twenty-three people and asked them to please go back to whatever they were really doing to make a living—selling shoes, driving cabs, working as accountants. They all had to have moonlighting jobs because what they had been doing in insurance certainly didn't count as a full-time job,

And, frankly, I think I rescued them. I helped them get back into whatever jobs they really should have been doing in the first place.

The previous agency manager never made any demands on them. I don't think they really resented the termination too much. I sent them back to occupations they probably could—and should—do better than what they had been doing at Phoenix. They weren't working there. They were just there.

But the three sales professionals I kept were important—because they had potential. Their problem was just that they lacked an effective manager. And when we started managing them, they produced spectacular results.

Before me, no manager ever came in earlier than they did, and no manager ever went home later.

So there I was coming in to work at 5 or 6 in the morning. And I stayed late at night to make up for the extra travel time. On the new job, if I got home at 8, it seemed early.

Being used to eighteen-hour days, I was having a picnic working only twelve or thirteen hours a day

These guys saw that I was working, so they started coming in a little bit earlier and going home a little bit later. And when their income started to reflect their stronger effort, they saw that what I was trying to teach them really did work.

I started to recruit new salespeople, and I was good at it. Sure, I guessed wrong many times each year, but I was slowly developing a great team. And the more they made, the more I made.

And even though things were going well, the company wasn't paying me enough to be a manager, so I had to go out and do my own personal production business. So here I was, coming in earlier, going home later, and it was still better than what I had been doing before, commuting to Connecticut every day.

The agents soon got the feeling that I was there to work, not to play, and so they decided to work harder.

There were lots of new agents coming in, lots of new people happening, lots of client calling. It was a flurry of activity, and the enthusiasm started to just permeate the walls, the carpet, the floor, the ceiling. Everybody started getting more enthusiastic and, frankly, it became an exponential spiral: the more enthusiastic we became, the more enthusiastic the environment became, which in turn made us *more* enthusiastic, which made it more . . .

It was just a wonderful, wonderful experience, creating that enthusiasm and watching it catch fire. And the truth is, to this day it hasn't stopped. We moved the office, but that same enthusiasm is still going strong, all over this place.

If I tell you anything in this book, I can tell you that you can set examples *for yourself* by what you do, by your own enthusiasm. Even if you have to fake it for a while. Do something enthusiastically and you'll be surprised at how you can actually train yourself. If you have enthusiasm, you'll exude it, and it will come back to you in spades.

If the people you pick to work with you don't want to participate in your enthusiasm, lose 'em. Get rid of 'em. Find those who will. Some people are what I call "sappers." No matter what you do or say, they find a way to sap your strength, tire you out, frustrate you. This isn't to say they aren't fine people. I'm just saying these are not the right people for you to be around. The chemistry is counterproductive.

Because, except in only the rarest of cases, you can't count on putting new spots on an existing leopard. It is better to get a leopard who has most of its spots in the right place already. In sales, you have no choice but to get rid of those leopards with the wrong spots. You can't fix them, no matter what you do.

So, what I strongly recommend is that you identify and work on your own brand of enthusiasm—and hang on to it throughout your life.

It can make things change for the better. It's worked for me.

Once we started recruiting new salespeople, and we started selling more insurance, and I realized I needed to make the income necessary to support my own lifestyle, everything seemed to fall in place.

The harder I worked, the luckier I got. I know it sounds trite, but that's exactly what happened.

But, remember, for me, this new arrangement in Philadelphia was an easier beat to walk. When I was travelling to get to work in Connecticut, I was still getting in by 6 A.M., but my day was so much longer then. So, while the agents here thought, "Wow, look at the hours this guy puts in!" They didn't realize that for me it was a break. I was getting it easier. It kept on going that way. I developed a certain inertia that I don't think I'll ever lose—as long as I keep pushing it along.

It's like if you are out of shape. It takes extra effort to get back into shape—but once you are in shape again, all you have to do is stick to your routine and you stay in shape. But sticking to the routine is easier than getting back into shape in the first place. That is one lucky thing I can say about myself: I've always known that I can never let up. Too many people make a habit of letting up, and it's hell to pay when they have to get back up to speed again. Oh, it can be done, of course. It's just so much harder than it is to keep the routine going.

In 1966 I was working my tail off, and my wife was totally supportive. My little girl, Lori, was born in July of that year, about the time we moved to Philadelphia.

I was encountering some stress then. I wanted to see clients and sell insurance, and I wanted to see agents and build an agency.

But I also wanted to see my wife and baby. There were only twenty-four hours in day. During the week, I was building the agency, and on the weekends and nights I was seeing clients. My wife got to see me when I came home for dinner, but my daughter, who was still asleep in the morning when I left for work, was always in bed by the time I got home. So, in order to see her, I took Lori out with me on Saturdays and Sundays when I would go see my clients. She was between three and five years old at that time.

On Saturday and Sundays, Lori and I would pick up the physician who would do the medical exams for my clients, and we'd go. If a client would object to seeing me with my daughter, then tough for that client—or potential client, I should say. I just wouldn't go. Lori was almost like my mascot.

It was like having a puppy with me. This little girl that was so cute and so precious, the people had to buy. That wasn't my original intention—not at all. But after a while, it became something wonderful. I hated to see her get older—just kidding!

We'd go to lunch before making our rounds. The doctor would bring my daughter lollipops, and then we'd be off to see clients. With all those clients buying, Lori caught the insurance enthusiasm—she grew up in it—and now she's in the business and knocking them dead. Maybe she learned it from me, or maybe she got it through osmosis from the lollipops that doctor gave her.

Occasionally, my wife would go with me, too. It was a regular family affair. Sue and I would lie around in bed on Sundays when we weren't working and dream up contests for our agents together. It was a joint effort that worked that way for at least six or seven years until we got the agency's momentum going full speed ahead.

If six or seven years seem like such a long time—believe me, it was. It was an eternity because we were starting from ground zero. It was like pushing a big, giant ball up a hill, and there are only two people to push it even though it requires one hundred. But the two people push the ball up the hill and can't stop for even one second, lest the ball run them over.

Sue and I worked together very hard, and nothing's really changed because we're working together right now, only a little differently. We do a little more networking, a little more different kinds of marketing than we were doing before, but we're still doing it now and it really hasn't changed.

I think the family, my kids, my wife, even my mom in Florida, all helped to build what we have now. I don't even pretend to take all the credit. Not even for a second.

More Trade Secrets

Client Research

On occasion I've ordered D&Bs (Dun & Bradstreet financial data reports) to help me assess a prospect. If you find a really strong individual with whom you really want to do business, it's worth it to have as much relevant information as possible. The D&B has information compiled in list form on an individual and is available for purchase.

The report will tell you when a prospect's company was founded, how much debt they currently have, what their lines of credit are, who the principals are. It gives you additional financial information on the company that can be of help in going into a meeting with a little bit more than the basic information. You'll probably want to go in knowing more than that someone is a good family man and an avid golfer.

I can order a D&B report and know more about my prospect, so that when I go there, I'm less of a stranger.

Use Enthusiasm!

How far would Dorothy have gotten without it?

1. Enthusiasm is an energy source.

It's like tapping into the local electric company. If you can keep enthusiasm going all the time, things will be charged up. Things will happen.

2. Enthusiasm creates an endless energy to achieve your goals.

If you can keep looking up and never look down, you have a better shot at achieving your goals. It's a priceless ingredient in every sale.

I don't know how it works, but the client can see through you. When you're happy and you're enthusiastic and you believe in what you're saying, the client believes in what you're saying. If you can make a presentation in which you appear totally convinced about your product's virtues, your enthusiasm will come through.

3. Enthusiasm builds courage.

I'm talking about the courage to do the right thing. Maybe doing the right thing means recommending a product that will be tougher to sell than some other product, but you know it is the right thing to do, so you do it!

Well, when you have enthusiasm, you can have that courage, that integrity. You can do what you have to do. Act enthusiastic and you'll be enthusiastic. In other words, act the role out.

Insight from Oz: Begin to behave like the person that you think you want to be. Then you may be struck with the brainstorm: What's the difference between acting like the person you want to be and actually being that person? The answer: nothing! It's the same thing, and you can begin doing it . . . immediately!

4. Nothing is as contagious as enthusiasm.

There used to be a sign popular in New York when I was growing up. Con Edison, the electric company, advertised the slogan: "Courtesy is contagious."

So is enthusiasm. Enthusiasm is contagious. And if you don't have it, you can give it to yourself just by faking it for a while.

The more enthusiastic you are, the more your prospect becomes enthusiastic. The more the prospect is, the more you become. And the more sales you make.

5. Enthusiasm is the cause of success, not the result.

In other words, you don't get enthusiastic because of success. You get successful because of enthusiasm, because you keep your energy level high.

Wearing rose-colored glasses does make a tremendous difference.

6. An enthusiastic salesperson expects to win.

Do you expect to win? When you go out to see somebody, do you expect that the end result is going to be a positive one? Because that's how you should approach it. Like in the card trick, if you are dead set on something, everything that happens can be interpreted as progress toward your goal. Most of the time, if you expect a positive outcome, you'll get it. Everyone has something to teach you. It's up to you to find out what that is and use it to further your cause.

Sacrifice = Reaching Your Goal

Dreaming and seeing the end result in mind. It's not simple and it's not easy.

It's a very big sacrifice that you have to make, and something that you really have to want.

You have to be prepared to pay the price. And measuring the cost is easy. It is measured in how many things you are willing to trade off—things you prefer to be doing—in exchange for plodding a few more inches toward your goal.

I think the price is very, very expensive. It was for me.

At some point in time I got very down, and I thought, "Darn it, I really don't know my kids. Maybe I'm a no-good father."

But I had to make some basic decisions for me, and I had to act on those decisions. If I was less than perfect, I admit it. But I did have my eye on a goal that I think wound up benefiting everyone in my family.

I don't think anything is for nothing. There's no free lunch; you have to buy everything you want; you have to buy a ticket. If you want success, if that's the journey you want—however you define it—and your success is to be extraordinary, not ordinary, you must do extraordinary things. You have to do the things that your counterparts at school or in business will never even consider doing. And most of those things that only extraordinary people do are in the realm of personal sacrifice.

Maybe it's something you don't even want to do. That's all right. You can be a happy, successful person without the extraordinary sacrifice. But you can't be an extraordinarily successful person. But not everyone needs—or wants—to be extraordinarily successful.

For me it wasn't a chore.

While it was hard work, it was part of the road map, part of my TripTik, to work twelve, thirteen hours a day.

The fact of the matter is, now, at sixty-four years of age, I'm still doing what I did then. It could be argued that when you love what you do—and that's another critical step, to find something you love to do—that you never really work a day in your life. And I don't think for a moment that I'm working. I just put time in toward the goal.

I don't see what I do all day as working. I'm having too much fun.

And because of the different things I do, whether it's speaking, running an agency, writing about business, or traveling, I don't have a chance to get bored, even though I'm putting in so much time. It's always fun.

As long as you keep your job exciting and keep being enthusiastic—that's the key.

It isn't easy to have the discipline, but having the excitement and the enthusiasm makes the discipline easier.

It's like taking orange juice with castor oil. You don't want castor oil, but castor oil's going to make you better, so you put some orange juice in to disguise it. You don't even know you're taking castor oil and then you get better, but you don't even know why. I guess that's what I'm doing. I find ways to mask the hard stuff with fun stuff.

Think Ahead

A checklist is important.

However, before you can start working your checklist, you first need to design it, to plan it.

So, one thing you need to do is to consult the pros. Whoever is the best in your field, find a way to consult them. Call them, meet with them, write to them, attend their speeches, read their articles or books. This book, in a sense, may help you develop a plan of action for what you want to accomplish.

So, the first thing you must determine is just exactly what it is you want.

1. Define the Desired Achievement

Take your typical commercial airplane pilot. He knows he has to fly from New York to Chicago. That's a major ingredient. If he doesn't know that he is going to go from New York to Chicago, he might go from New York to St. Louis instead.

He wants to go to Chicago because that was what his flight plan called for.

He even knows the exact moment his wheels will touch down in Chicago before he leaves New York. He knows how fast to fly, what route to fly.

Now, I'm assuming you want to do a certain amount of personal sales. Whether it's life insurance or car manufacturing or fixing shoes, I don't care.

The fact of the matter is that before you begin, you must know what you want to accomplish. Once you've got that done, determine what is required to get you there.

2. Develop a Checklist

Now, you're old enough and smart enough to know what has to be done in a given situation. If you don't know, try it the first time, make a couple of mistakes, and make corrections as you go along.

Let's say you decide you want to sell a client a certain product. You put things together in a proposal, but the client doesn't buy.

Well, you have to do what all pros do. You sit down, figure out what—if anything—went wrong, and you modify your plan.

Find out why he didn't buy and what must you do to fix the proposal, so that next time you see a client in the same circumstances as the person who didn't buy, you'll have a better chance.

Also, don't forget to analyze your successes. If he *did* buy, what did you say right that made him buy? How can you get him—and others—to do it again?

So, you want to develop your own checklist based on things that you actually experience, either at your desk or out in the field.

Don't just be content to say, "Well, I got a sale! Hip, hip, hooray!" Make sure you know why you made that sale—so you can be sure to do it again.

3. Prioritize

Of all the things I need to do, which should I do first? Where am I now? That's the third step.

It's a question of putting your priorities in order. Are you doing the right thing at the right time?

Determine where you are and where you want to go.

Are both those ideas in concert? Is where you are now on a direct path to where you want to go? Is it a doable route? Can you get there? Are there any known obstacles?

If you can, develop the specific action steps that you must complete in order to get there—and what are the steps? Look at the steps to get there and figure out how long will it take.

Can you keep the end in mind? Do you know what the end result looks like?

That's a very important point.

In order to get to the end, you must know clearly what the end looks like so every step you take is toward that goal, and you must ask yourself every time—is what you are doing now getting you one step closer to the goal you want to reach?

If it's not, you either have the wrong goal or you are in the wrong place.

You may have a good idea for something to do, but if it doesn't fit your goal, there's no point. Go back to the captain's example. He might think it's a wonderful idea to fly toward St. Louis to look down upon the arch there—except that if his flight plan directs him to Chicago, the St. Louis thought is not a very good idea.

He's dressed in the wrong suit for the right occasion.

So, in my opinion, the whole concept of where are you now versus where you want to go is more important than what steps you decide to take to get you there.

4. Goal Posts and Landmarks

Goalposts or landmarks will be your most important helpers along the way.

What are the goalposts or landmarks along the way? How do you know that your journey is going in the right direction? You have to keep looking back and say, "Is what I just did going to get me closer to where I want to go?"

If it doesn't, you made a wrong turn. If it does, you're on the right track.

How do you know when you're done? How will you know when you've got the task completed? Some things aren't clear cut. Ask anyone who's ever cooked a Thanksgiving turkey. How did they know the bird was finished? They knew the signs.

They knew what to look for, either from their own experience or from what someone else told them.

More Trade Secrets

Hiring a Good Secretary

You'll be surprised how effectively you can delegate things—and how doing so frees you to do more profitable things.

A good secretary is invaluable.

You can't find and train a good secretary—you have to steal one.

You must steal a secretary. If you are in action, if you are really doing business, you haven't got the time it takes to get somebody who is green, train them, and make them yours.

It will slow you down too much.

Find the best secretary in the city—in any field, it doesn't have to be your field—and steal that person. Hire her—or him—for a few bucks more and get one.

With an experienced person, you'll be up and running in a matter of minutes rather than months.

Criteria for a Good Secretary

You want somebody who's disciplined, someone who is also very good, somebody who wants to take her/his boss to the next level.

For example, if you have won some sales awards and you want to win your region's top sales spot, you want to find a secretary who wants to have a boss who wants to go to the top, too—and is disciplined enough to take you there. There are plenty of people out there who are willing to help you get there. The trick is finding them.

Frankly, if that person is really good, she can make you so busy, make you so effective, that you'll go to the next level of success. That's why you need a good person working with you, doing all the things you can't, should not, or don't want to do.

Insight from Oz: If you are making $75 an hour and the secretary is making $20 an hour, who should do a task that you are both capable of doing? Find the best way to do it and push that task down the ladder of administrative costs, down to the cheapest way you have to get that job done well.

Your secretary has to know what you expect of her, and you must know what she expects of you. It's a two-way street.

For me, I use a forty-point checklist that lays out everything my secretary needs to know about my travel preferences.

When I travel, my secretary knows where on the plane I like to sit, she knows what time of day I like to travel, what class of travel I want to go on, and what I want to do when I arrive at my destination.

And because of that, we spend very little time talking about it. Now she only books my trips the way I want them booked.

How much more efficient would you be if all you had to do was say, "Hey, Rosemary! Seattle next Thursday." End of discussion, and everything will be perfect, just the way you want it. How much is that worth?

And it is all possible because I took the time to develop my forty-point checklist that describes exactly what I want.

Words from the Wise
Valuable Insights about the Journey—from Successful People

I am an attorney who specializes in corporate and securities work. In this line of business, you might assume that I don't develop close relationships with clients—but you'd be wrong.

When dealing with clients, you have to make them feel like they are truly important. And whether they are or not, you have to make them feel that way, particularly if you are in a service business. You have to appear as if it being with that person is most important thing in the world.

Aside from courteous and friendly service, you have to be genuinely concerned about what a client needs and wants. Usually, they want—and deserve—immediate service.

Many times business people have told me that they are too tied up to help me.

No matter what you do, always avoid using the phrase, "I'm too busy." It is a horrible thing to say to someone. You can always increase staff levels to handle new work if you get too busy, but you can't take back having insulted someone by making them feel like they don't matter.

Something else that is important: there is a tendency of professionals to tell clients why a certain thing just can't get done—or why it might not be a good idea. The successful professionals are those who find the way to do it. Being creative in finding ways to get things done is a key to my success.

—Ramon R. Obod

Get Going—Kansas May
Be Closer Than You Think!

Get going!
You already know you want to do.
You know you can't stop.
You know you have to do all the little things we talked about to make it all work.

It's morning. It's time to go. You wake up. You had this wonderful dream. You have to put it on paper. It's the plan.

Get going!

All of the material in this book are what you need for preparation: the dreaming up of a goal, the thinking about it, the looking at it, the punching it up, the mapping it out.

Here is where you pull the trigger. Here is where you actually *get going!*

This section shows you how to release all the energy to make all those dreams and hopes come true. You can't do what we talk about in this section until you've spent time on the ideas that came earlier.

As you do them, one piece at a time, you're developing the road map to make it happen.

You inhabit a world where so few people actually have the courage to get going and keep going. So, the one thing that makes the ideas in this book so amazing is that if you do the things we talk about, it'll make you special. You will truly be one in a million.

But most people just won't do it! I can't explain why. I can just report my own experience working with thousands of salespeople.

Insight from Oz: And it is so simple if you will only stop and break the giant challenges ahead of you into smaller, less overwhelming pieces!

Begin to Move Forward and Never, Ever
Let Up. An Object in Motion Stays in Motion

Wizard Wisdom: Sufi mystics give this advice to their students who are on the road to enlightenment: "Begin, continue, and do not ever stop."

Never let up.

How many obstacles does Dorothy encounter?

There is a price for success, and it is always paid in advance. In other words, you have to pay *before* you pump. You have to keep doing it and doing it until it finally pays off . . . and, one way or another, it always pays off.

Now, you ask, how can you be that one in a million?

How successful do you really want to be? And maybe it's not one in one million, maybe it's one in one hundred thousand. I never counted! Who cares!

The point is, you *can* be that person.

Now, as you've already seen, it isn't very difficult.

This isn't really tough stuff. This isn't the kind of technical challenge faced by genetic engineers, and it isn't the artistic challenge faced by Michelangelo. It is the personal challenge that you are facing right now. And you can succeed. All you need to do is to begin—and to continue.

You can get *whatever it is you want* as long you do these steps.

So if you know these steps are so easy, and if other people know these steps are easy, and if other successful people have been saying essentially the same things for centuries, why won't everybody do it?

They don't really want to be where they say they want to be.

They won't buy the ticket because they're not willing to pay the price.

Get going is pressing the Start button, holding on tight, and never letting go until you get what you want.

But it's not just reaching one goal. It's reaching all the goals you establish for the rest of your life.

And it's that one thousand months Nature's allotted to you. It's getting what you want over and over and over and over again. Dreaming, it, planning it, working it, and finally getting it.

Last Comes First

Think of *the end result* all the time.

This is so important that I want to repeat it.

This sets the stage for your success.

You have to begin the task with the end in mind. If you can do that, you know what you're going to experience.

It's like the Nike sneaker ads advise: "Just Do It."

Get it going. Start doing it. I guarantee you'll get swept up in it and find yourself at the other end sooner than you think.

How do you get to the other end?

Start.

Get going.

Work the process. The process is as important as the end.

If you don't perform the activities that make up the process, there will be no end.

Checklist Reminder

There's something else so critical to your success that I want to emphasize it by telling you this story:

The other morning, while talking to the young people in an agency meeting here, I described to them a wonderful, wonderful experience I had just had.

What happened was this: Last week I was in Europe, and I had to leave my hotel at 5 in the morning to make an 8:05 plane from Interlaken to Zurich. I got to the airport at about 7 for an 8:05 plane. I got to the airport early, I changed my tickets, and I did what I had to do and got on the plane that was going from Zurich to Paris, a one-hour-and-five-minute trip. I love to fly.

Now, many, many years ago, before I lost sight in one of my eyes, I had learned to be a pilot and I learned the discipline of flying, but I never got to finish the pilot-license training because in the midst of it all, I became partially blind and couldn't fly anymore. But I still love the idea of flying.

Well, I got into the airplane twenty minutes early, so I asked the flight attendant in the front, "Why don't they have first class in Europe anymore?"

"We don't do it and we haven't done it for eight or nine years," she replied. "People just don't want to pay for the service. The best you can get is business class."

Now, I believe in always flying first class. Here's why. If you are flying anyway, then you have to have a ticket. So you've already paid for most of a first-class seat. So the question is, is it worth the extra money to sit in first-class? Absolutely! Think of whom you are likely to sit next to there: extremely successful people, business leaders, prosperous professionals—exactly the kind of people you want to meet.

There is another interesting thing about flying in Europe. They do not close the captain's door to the cockpit. While you're in the air, the door's open all the time. In the United States, for security reasons, that door not only has to be closed but also has to be locked. But this door was wide open. I could see the captain sitting down. I got up, walked forward, and looked into the cockpit. "Hi," I said. "Hi," he said, right back.

Well, we started talking. "My God, this is a brand-new plane," I said. "How old is it?"

"It's probably a year and a half old, maybe less," the captain said in a charming French accent. That was when I noticed that only two pilots were flying the plane.

"Yes," he said. "There's only two of us now. We don't need any more. Used to be four people. Now there's only two."

"That's interesting," I said. "This is a very big plane for just two people to control, and you seem like you're on kings' thrones in there. You're in big chairs instead of being squeezed in, and you have this wonderful panel full of dozens of electronic things. But something's missing." I had looked all over the control panel. "Where is your steering wheel? You don't have one!"

"Yes, we do," he said, putting his hand on this tiny joystick— smaller than most of the ones you see little kids play with in toy stores. "I fly the plane with this."

Well, I said good-bye and went back to my seat, and in a few minutes we took off. While we were en route, the stewardess approached me and said, "The captain said that if you would like, on descent, you can come into the cockpit."

"Oh sure!" I said. "I would love to do that."

So I finished up my breakfast as quickly as I could. Taking my tray away, the stewardess said, "Come with me now, Mr. Friedman. I'll take you to the captain."

And off I went. I walked into the cockpit and saw that there were only two chairs.

"Where do you want me to sit?" I asked the captain.

"Excuse me!" he laughed and reached between him and the copilot to pull out a little jumpseat that had been folded somewhere down there. The stewardess adjusted the seat and strapped me in.

Now, here were these two guys sitting in these gigantic thrones, and then there was me, in this little baby seat.

"In a few minutes, we'll begin our descent, Mr. Friedman," said the captain. "Are you comfortable?"

"Yes, I'm very comfortable.

"Are you happy?"

"Deliriously happy," I said. It was true.

Then we began the descent. Everything was computerized, the captain explained. Everything was automatic—computer-programmed—and backed up by secondary systems, which in turn were backed up with even more equipment. It would have been a shot of ten million to one that anything could go wrong, the captain told me. This plane could have landed without any human help, except that the captain wanted to land it manually.

As we went along, I asked, "How soon until we begin our descent?"

At that moment, the captain and copilot picked up clipboards and started talking to each other. The pilot didn't answer me.

It was most interesting how this plane was operating because we were in total fog. You couldn't see a single thing at twenty thousand feet.

Now, the whole point of this story (besides me being very happy in the plane and watching them land it)—is that the captain and copilot each had a checklist with about 150 items.

I could hear the control tower in Orle say something in French to the captain, and he said something back.

Sitting there, I began talking again, and the captain said, "Oh, Mr. Friedman, do not talk now!"

They were speaking to each other in French about things necessary for the landing process. Nothing could get in their way, not even the guest whom they were trying to be nice to.

Then the captain and his copilot began ticking off the items on the checklist in response to something the tower said. And for every item the captain said something about, the copilot repeated it. Then the tower would say something else. Then the captain repeated it. Then the copilot. I didn't know what they were saying, but once they started, they didn't stop. It was all business. Very serious stuff. No joking around, no side remarks (as far as I could tell), just item after item, ba-dee-boop, ba-dee-boop, click, click, click, ba-dee-boop, ba-dee-boop, click, click, click, ba-dee-boop, ba-dee-boop, click, click, click.

They kept doing this up and down those clipboards for the entire descent, which took maybe about nine or ten minutes until we finally broke through the fog. All the way down to four hundred feet, there was zero visibility. Just thick fog. It didn't phase them.

Not once during the entire descent did the pilot even look outside. He didn't have to. He had all the information he needed very clearly organized, just when he needed it. It was an exercise in total discipline. At that time, that checklist was their god.

When we finally touched down and I sensed it was OK to talk again, I asked, "Why do you have to have the tower say it to you, you say it back to the tower, refer to your checklist, tell the copilot what you're doing, he says something, and tells you? What's the point of all that?"

"Because, Mr. Friedman, " he said, "we very much do not like to crash."

So, isn't that the story of life in the first place?

Nobody likes crashing (airplanes or farmhouses!), yet every day we do not use the discipline and the checklists that this captain and copilot and the tower used, and so we crash a lot.

It was just totally wonderful to watch them work because nothing at all was left to chance. So, one of the things I would suggest to you is that you be as determined and focused as they were during the descent.

Nothing got in the way of their mission of landing that plane safely, and I see a definite corollary between success and that plane landing. You must have a checklist of what you're going to do, and then you have to do it—and let nothing, absolutely nothing, get in your way.

If there's a mountain in your way, go through it, over it, or around it. Dig a tunnel under it if you have to, but do the things on your checklist.

Wizard Wisdom: When some emergency comes up that causes you to temporarily abandon your checklist, don't worry. But make a superhuman effort to get back on track as soon as the emergency is over.

Great Scene #12

Dorothy wakes up in her own bed, surrounded by those who love her. Like the rest of us, life makes Dorothy older and wiser. And she learns that there really is no place like home.

Dorothy's Kansas is happening now. She wakes up to the familiar sounds and smells of home. The Technicolor is gone. Everything is in black and white and shades of gray.

Auntie Em is there, pleading with Dorothy to wake up.

Aunt Em and Uncle Henry hover over her nervously.

Professor Marvel shows up to look in on Dorothy, saying he's come by because he heard the little girl has sustained a big bump on her head from the storm.

Dorothy hears this and is confused by her dream about Oz. She knows it was real, yet there were so many similarities between Oz and Kansas. She can't figure it out.

The three farmhands arrive and gather around the bed. Dorothy tries to convince them it wasn't a dream at all. They try to explain to her how real dreams can seem to be.

They all laugh.

Toto jumps up on the bed to be with Dorothy. Dorothy speaks to him, saying that no matter what has happened, they are now home. In their room. And everyone is there. She says she loves them all and that she'll never leave them again, ever. Once again, she says that there is no place like home.

"Auntie Em, there really is no place like home."

Well, folks. I don't think I could have said it any better.
"Auntie Em, there really is no place like home."

Understanding Your Own Unconscious Mind

How successful do you really, *really* want be?

If you are not yet where you want to be in life, in any respect—money, relationships, sense of accomplishment—right where you are *right now* is the perfect place to start.

Before I began to achieve success, I didn't know that my unconscious mind had a different agenda than my conscious mind. They seemed to suffer from a failure to communicate with each other, and I got caught in the middle of the tug of war. It was counterproductive.

Think about Dorothy's unconscious. She was a young, vibrant girl, full of energy and dreams and desire—stuck on a poor and dusty farm in rural Kansas. It's true she loved her family and friends, but still, there was a definite gloomy quality to her environment.

Maybe, in her young, inexperienced mind, she worried that she lacked the courage, brains, and heart to achieve whatever dreams she was going to have for herself.

So, doesn't it make sense that in Oz—in her dream state there—that she "meets" a Scarecrow who thinks he lacks intelligence, a Lion known only for his cowardice, and a Tin Man who thinks he is incapable of love?

And in going through the trials that she and they experience, she comes to be tremendously self-confident, and she comes to believe in her mind and her heart and her courage.

When it comes to understanding your own unconscious perceptions, you need to start by learning to "hear" what your subconscious mind is saying. You need to learn to eavesdrop on your subconscious.

I do it by paying attention to what's going on in my belly.

And I don't mean digestively, either.

I mean I use my belly as a gauge to help me make decisions. The belly seems to have a direct line into the subconscious. When things are wrong, I feel it in my belly before I think it in my head. And if I'm consciously nervous about something, but don't feel it in my gut, then I tend to think I'm worried about nothing.

When you can get your conscious mind and subconscious mind working together toward the same goal, you have a very tough hand to beat. You're closing in on success.

If you can't outwit your subconscious in your head, you have to do it in your belly.

Your head says your going to do something, but your belly reads your subconscious that says, "Forget it, I'm not going to try. Don't even bother."

It's your subconscious mind that wants you to sleep late, procrastinate, avoid the tough decisions, isn't it? Do you *consciously* want to do what you know is right? Well, when you are constantly being sidetracked by your own behavior, look to your subconscious mind if you want to see the culprit.

As soon as you show your unconscious who's boss, that's when you'll begin succeeding.

Time to Click Your Heels!

Dear Reader,

Thank you for spending so much of your invaluable time with me and Dorothy and the rest of the crew.

You may be highly psyched right now to get going and to take the first step down the Yellow Brick Road you've devised for yourself.

So, I'll let you go—right after this superquick review.

Take these ten steps for success . . . down the Yellow Brick Road:

1. *Struggle a little.* It won't kill you. Dorothy does. Easy jobs don't pay very much. That is why sales jobs can pay big money. Jobs that pay for results—not time and effort—pay big money.

2. *Never let up.* How many obstacles does Dorothy encounter? There is a price for success, and it is always paid in advance. You have to keep doing it and doing it and doing it until it finally pays off . . . and it always pays off.

3. Keep in mind that striving for success is like climbing a mountain: **do it one step at a time.** Envision the size of the mountain, know how many steps it takes, get all the things you need for mountain climbing, then all of a sudden, next thing you know, you are on top! Struggle for success, not mediocrity.

4. *Enjoy today but prepare for tomorrow.* Remember, success is a journey, not a destination. Have fun while you are doing it. Sing and dance and skip down the road. Make sure that every day is the best it can be.

5. *Ask for help. People rarely succeed alone.* Scarecrows, Lions, Tin Men, Munchkins, Wizards —there's always a team and always somebody that helps. Find that person who can help you, and there you go.

178

6. *Find a mentor.* Learn from those people around you—even if it turns out to be a little dog. Look at those who are successful, emulate what they do, and then do it as well.

7. *Go the extra mile.* Successful people make a habit of doing those things that unsuccessful people won't do. You have to do things that nobody else will do. When you do them, you become different. Promise a lot and deliver even more! And remember the motto of life: don't copy—create. Do something nobody else is doing.

8. *Do it now.* Successful people pay a price for success, and it's usually in time—or in the risks you take. It's in doing what has to be done today and not tomorrow.

9. *Always begin with the end in mind.* Know that you want to end up in Kansas. The past is history. Learn from it for today. Stop looking back, only look forward. Begin today making a brand-new ending.

10. *Believe in yourself.* You have everything you need inside you. Nobody can make you inferior without your consent. You are in charge of you, every single day of your life.

OK, so there's one more: **get started!** You're off to see your Wizard!

And, if you wish, please write to me and let me know how *The Wonderful Wizard in You!* has helped you in your journey to Success. Good luck!

Sid Friedman

A Few Great Books
That Helped Change My Life

Benson, Herbert. *Relaxation Response.* New York, N.Y.: Morrow, 1975.

Maltz, Maxwell. *Psycho-Cybernetics.* North Hollywood, Calif.: Wilshire, 1973.

Mandino, Og. *The Greatest Salesman in the World.* Hollywood, Fla.: Lifetime Books, 1992.

Peale, Norman Vincent. *The Power of Positive Thinking.* New York, N.Y.: Fawcett, 1996.

Thompson, Andrew H. *The Feldman Method: The Words and Working Philosophy of the World's Greatest Insurance Salesman.* Chicago, Ill.: Longman Financial Services Publications, 1989.

The Beginning